Keeping Up with Emerging Technologies

Keeping Up with Emerging Technologies

Best Practices for Information Professionals

Nicole Hennig

LIBRARIES UNLIMITED™

An Imprint of ABC-CLIO, LLC

Santa Barbara, California • Denver, Colorado

Library of Congress Cataloging-in-Publication Data

Names: Hennig, Nicole, author.
Title: Keeping up with emerging technologies : best practices for information professionals / Nicole Hennig.
Description: Santa Barbara, California : Libraries Unlimited, an imprint of ABC-CLIO, LLC, [2017] | Includes bibliographical references and index.
Identifiers: LCCN 2017008846 (print) | LCCN 2017021555 (ebook) | ISBN 9781440854415 (ebook) | ISBN 9781440854408 (acid-free paper)
Subjects: LCSH: Librarians–Effect of technological innovations on. | Technological literacy. | Technological innovations–Information resources. | Information technology–Information resources. | Libraries–Information technology–Planning. | Libraries–Information technology–Evaluation. | Public services (Libraries) | Library users–Effect of technological innovations on.
Classification: LCC Z682.35.T43 (ebook) | LCC Z682.35.T43 H46 2017 (print) | DDC 025.00285—dc23
LC record available at https:/lccn.loc.gov/2017008846

ISBN: 978–1–4408–5440–8
EISBN: 978–1–4408–5441–5

21 20 19 18 17   1 2 3 4 5

This book is also available as an eBook.

Libraries Unlimited
An Imprint of ABC-CLIO, LLC

ABC-CLIO, LLC
130 Cremona Drive, P.O. Box 1911
Santa Barbara, California 93116-1911
www.abc-clio.com

This book is printed on acid-free paper ∞

Manufactured in the United States of America

Contents

Acknowledgments

I would like to thank my colleagues at the MIT Libraries, where from 1999 through 2013 I had the pleasure of working with so many smart, engaging, and creative library professionals. I would especially like to thank Nina Davis-Mills and Steven Gass, who approved my many requests for conference attendance, continuing education, and budgets for experimenting with new technologies. I would also like to thank our user experience group—a group that excelled at working together as a new department and had so much passion for improving library services for the MIT community. Thank you!

CHAPTER 1

Introduction

Why This Book?

If you've been an information professional for any length of time, you've certainly heard over and over that technology is changing quickly and exponentially, and that it's very difficult to keep up. It's a very popular topic for articles, workshops, conference sessions, and books.

You've probably felt overwhelmed at times and struggled to keep up with the flow of information about new technologies. You've seen trends come and go, and wondered how and where to invest your limited time and budget.

You might have a position in your organization for an "emerging technologies librarian," or something similar. If not, that role might be a part of other job roles that you or your colleagues have. You might need to write job descriptions for those kinds of positions. Or you might be a student in library school with an interest in technology positions in libraries—maybe you want to become the person your colleagues rely on for keeping up. This book is for all of you.

Just about every source I've seen on this topic aims to inform readers about specific trends and technologies coming in the near future. These are quite useful and they often include a section or chapter on how to keep up.[1] You can also find journal articles or conference talks with specific tips and techniques for keeping up.[2] But it can be hard to find one complete resource that brings together *methods* for keeping up and bringing new technologies into your service offerings.

This book aims to consolidate those methods in one place. It will begin by covering techniques for gathering information about emerging technologies and about user needs. I'll recommend several types of resources to follow and I'll discuss strategies for finding time to keep up with all of this information in the midst of your busy life.

Since every librarian has different skills, talents, temperaments, and roles to play, I'm going to suggest that we use two broad categories of skills in order to discuss this kind of work: visionaries and implementers. I'll define those two types, and discuss how to use these skills sets in complementary ways in your organization.

Next, I'll recommend sources for following ethical debates about new technologies, aligning your work for inclusiveness, considering diversity and accessibility, and considering the digital divide.

We'll then look at methods for evaluating and analyzing what you've found, matching technologies with user needs, designing small experiments and evaluating the results, presenting to and persuading decision-makers, and passing on projects to implementers.

Chapters 2–8 of this book are a catalog of methods, resources, and strategies. In Chapter 9 of this book, we'll look at how to define the role of "emerging technologies librarian," along with skills and talents needed, and sample job descriptions. I'll include what to do if you are a small organization or a one-person library.

In Chapter 11, I'll conclude with a bibliography of books, blogs, articles, and websites for learning more. At the end, I've included a guide to some of the best mobile apps for doing this kind of work.

This book is designed so that you can go back and refer to the chapters you care about most, as you're doing this type of work. My hope is that this handbook will be useful for years to come, no matter which technologies are on the horizon.

The good news is that it *is* possible to deal with the information deluge without feeling constantly overwhelmed. In my 14 years working at the MIT Libraries (first as web manager/usability specialist, then as head of the user experience department), I had a chance to try out many different methods and techniques, and to benefit from the ideas of experts outside of our field. In this book, I've brought together all of the most useful methods (tried and tested), in order to make this information easy to use in your library.

When you have a plan and a set of methods like these, you can design library programs and services that make a strong positive difference in the lives of your users. And you can keep up with the fast changing world of new technologies.

Visionaries and Implementers: Two Roles for This Work

I'd like to begin by discussing some of the skills, talents, and temperaments that are best for this kind of work. Depending on how big or small your organization is, you can divide these skills into different roles for different people.

There are some skills and talents that are useful for all of us to have, and others that might be best split into different roles: visionary versus implementer.

Often there are people who excel at visionary and creative thinking, but have no patience for the details of implementation. There are others who are great at managing large projects, keeping track of every detail, and focusing on getting everything done. They may not be so good at creative, visionary thinking. You probably know specific people who match these types. These skills and temperaments overlap in many people—so perhaps it's better viewed as a continuum. Think about where you fall on that continuum.

Of course, there are qualities and skills that are important for all information professionals to have. The skills include the following:

- A strong sense of empathy for users
- Knowing how to work well with diverse groups of people
- A love of continuous learning
- Being good at teamwork and collaboration
- Being an effective communicator

Other skills may fit better into separately defined roles: roles such as "visionary" or "implementer." I'm using these terms in a broad way, recognizing that most people don't fit completely into only one or the other set of qualities. Most of us are somewhere on a continuum between them (Figure 1.1).

Visionary   **Implementer**

Figure 1.1: Visionary and implementer—a continuum

I'd also like to say that neither of these sets of skills is more important than the other, even though so-called "visionaries" are often glamorized in our culture.[3] Both roles are vital in order to bring new ideas from vision to implementation.

Here are some characteristics of each role or type.

The Visionary

- has the ability to look at the big picture without getting bogged down in details.
- does not easily get overwhelmed when faced with a deluge of information.
- is good at thinking creatively and combining ideas from different fields.
- has a desire to be an "early adopter" (taking it in stride if things break).
- has a strong curiosity about emerging technologies and where they might lead.
- has a sense of optimism about the possibilities of new technologies.
- is a continual learner, with a love for learning about new technologies.
- is good at communicating in interesting ways that grab your emotions as well as your intellect.

The Implementer

- is good at analyzing and understanding specific details.
- is good at evaluating and organizing information.
- is good at applying the results of user needs studies.
- prefers to use new technologies after others have tested them and they are more mature and more solid.
- is good at thinking linearly and understanding cause and effect.
- has a healthy skepticism about new technologies and possible pitfalls.
- asks interesting questions about each new technology.
- is good at project management, leading teams, and making sure details get carried out correctly.

One problem that sometimes arises is that, within one role or one job description, the people in technology roles are supposed to be good at all of those things—or a mixture of things from opposite sides of the continuum. I'd like to suggest that we try to group these skill sets or talents into different job roles, with the role of "emerging technologies librarian" focusing on the visionary side of the continuum.

If you are a small organization or a one-person library, you might need all of those skills at different times. However, it's a very good idea if you can be aware of these differences and take advantage of splitting these roles when you can—letting the visionary and the implementer each work at what they are best at. If you are working alone, you can partner with others temporarily or engage consultants with the skills on the other side of the continuum from you.

I'll revisit these skills later in this book when we look at how to define the role of "emerging technologies librarian." I'll also offer strategies for how to use the tips in this book differently, depending on where you see yourself in this continuum.

Challenges for Libraries: Technology Staffing

Almost every position in libraries these days needs technology skills as part of the job. If you look at current job listings, you'll see that many job descriptions emphasize trend-spotting and knowledge of emerging technology trends.

In a 2015 NMC Horizon Report: Library Edition, one of the challenges identified was "Rethinking the Roles and Skills of Librarians."[4] This was listed in the section called "Difficult challenges: Those that we understand but for which solutions are elusive."

According to the report:

> Many libraries are in the midst of rearranging their organizations, resulting in the creation of new departments, positions, and responsibilities for library professionals. Indeed, more than half the advertised positions in recent years have been for newly created or significantly redefined roles. *There is a clear hiring trend that emphasizes finding more functional specialists that have a strong digital or technology background* [emphasis mine]. The challenge is in building capacity for these new specialized roles and providing sufficient training along the way.[5]

The report also gives statistics about the increasing trend for job listings to require significant technical skills or to be completely technology-focused. According to another report (from San Jose State University in spring 2016) about job trends in libraries,

> Employers want candidates who are adept at trend spotting, cognizant of emerging trends and technologies, and skilled at analyzing and implementing new trends and technologies. Stay current and informed of new developments in the LIS field as well as general business and technology trends.[6]

The Roles and Responsibilities of "Emerging Technologies Librarians" Are Quite Varied

In order to meet this need of keeping up with new technologies, many libraries have created a position for an "emerging technologies librarian," or have included that role as part of other job descriptions.

But the role of "emerging technologies librarian" is often not clearly defined. In 2013, an interesting paper was published by Tara Radniecki called "Study on Emerging Technologies Librarians: How a New Library Position and Its Competencies Are Evolving to Meet the Technology and Information Needs of Libraries and Their Patrons."[7] Her study aimed to determine what the roles, responsibilities, and competencies of emerging technology librarians included. She did two things: analyzed job advertisements (via ALA's JobLIST database from the previous six years) and conducted a survey of emerging technologies librarians.

What she found was that these roles were practiced in a wide variety of ways, with a wide variety of skill sets. Most of her survey respondents reported a discrepancy between their jobs as they were defined and what they did in practice. She came up with the following list of categories from her analysis of the job descriptions.

- Trendspotting and implementation
- Website management
- Reference activities
- Information literacy and instruction
- Collaboration with internal and external groups
- Liaison to academic department
- Creating online instruction materials
- Technology assessment
- Social media/Web 2.0/Outreach

- Technology training for both staff and patrons
- Electronic resource management
- IT/systems
- Work toward tenure and promotion
- Digital initiatives
- Electronic resource management
- Supervisory
- Online reference services and collections
- Equipment and e-classroom management[8]

She concluded that it wasn't possible from this study to determine a set of competencies because of all these differences. So she called for further studies to be done.

> As with many newly created positions, the exact roles and responsibilities of the emerging technologies librarian remain varied and vague. This leaves library administration unsure if they would benefit from creating the position, prospective emerging technologies librarians unsure of what skills and competencies they will need, and current emerging technologies librarians feeling disconnected and without clear direction.[9]

You're probably not surprised at this if you've worked in libraries for any length of time. It's a common problem for libraries to be short-staffed, and to need to combine several sets of duties in one job description. Given that we often may not have the staff or budgeting to create many new positions, it's a reality that this kind of work will usually need to be combined with existing roles.

So, how can we clearly define this type of work, and what types of skills and qualities are needed for it? That is a topic I will cover in depth in Chapter 9.

So in closing:

a. There is a growing need for technology-focused jobs in libraries.
b. Many job postings emphasize trend-spotting and knowledge of emerging technology trends.
c. There is a trend toward hiring "emerging technologies librarians," or including that role as a significant part of another job description.

But the job descriptions are all over the map, and the role of "emerging technologies librarian" is often not clearly defined.

In chapter 9, we'll look at some current job descriptions to see how they are defined and what other roles they are combined with. I'll then suggest some ways to effectively define and divide this type of work, along the lines of what we've already discussed about "visionaries" versus "implementers."

For now, think about where you fit on the continuum of visionaries versus implementers, and read on for strategies and resources for keeping up.

Endnotes

1. See the bibliography at the end of this book for some recommended books for librarians about specific emerging technologies.

2. Such as this presentation by Jennifer Koerber, "Emerging Technologies for Librarians: Keeping Up & Staying Fresh," January 28, 2016, http://www.slideshare.net/JenniferKoerber/emerging-technologies-for-librarians-keeping-up-staying-fresh.

3. For an interesting essay about this, see Andrew Russell and Lee Vinsel, "Hail the Maintainers," accessed January 8, 2017, https://aeon.co/essays/innovation-is-overvalued-maintenance-often-matters-more.

4. NMC Horizon Report, Library Edition, 2015, 28–29, http://cdn.nmc.org/media/2015-nmc-horizon-report-library-EN.pdf.

5. Ibid., 28.

6. Jennifer M. Overaa, "Emerging Career Trends for Information Professionals: A Snapshot of Job Postings," Spring 2016, SJSU School of Information, http://ischool.sjsu.edu/sites/default/files/content_pdf/career_trends.pdf, slide 28.

7. Tara Radniecki, "Study on Emerging Technologies Librarians: How a New Library Position and Its Competencies Are Evolving to Meet the Technology and Information Needs of Libraries and Their Patrons," Paper presented at: IFLA WLIC 2013—Singapore—Future Libraries: Infinite Possibilities in Session 152—Reference and Information Services, http://library.ifla.org/id/eprint/134.

8. Ibid., 5.

9. Ibid., 14.

CHAPTER 2

Gathering Information: Sources and Strategies

Introduction

The next few chapters are about gathering information from a wide variety of sources. It's not about going in depth, or evaluating information—yet. We'll look at different types of information to scan and track, with ideas about how to deal with information overload.

You sometimes hear the argument that we need to begin with users—their needs and desires—before we look at which technologies might best serve them. While it is essential to understand the needs of our users, it's also important to keep up with emerging technologies, in order to come up with innovative ideas that meet the needs of your users.

If you don't know what's possible with new technologies, you can't match them up with user needs. Usually, the best ideas for uses of new technologies emerge out of experimentation with them.

I recommend keeping up with new technologies and with user needs at the same time, or in an alternating fashion. I'll go more into depth about ways to understand user needs and match them with technologies in an upcoming chapter. For now, we'll focus on scanning the environment for new technology ideas.

Skimming and Scanning

Skimming and scanning is a great skill to have. There is never going to be enough time to read or watch everything you're interested in. You can learn a lot from book reviews, free e-book samples, and articles that you've skimmed. You can do this in spare moments, like when you're in public transportation, during breaks or lunch, or while exercising and listening to audio podcasts about new technologies.

Your goal at this stage is to get a sense of what's coming and what's being talked about. It's not yet the time for in-depth understanding, or evaluating information.

Some experts say, and I agree, that "people who know how to skim and scan are flexible readers. They read according to their purpose and get the information they need quickly without wasting time. They do not read everything, which is what increases their reading speed. Their skill lies in knowing what specific information to read and which method to use."[1]

If you set up various channels of information to come to you automatically on a regular basis, you can process information quickly, and save items for reading, watching, or listening later. For example, you can subscribe to e-mail newsletters, blogs, podcasts, video channels, Twitter feeds and lists, and so on. The trick is to find the best sources for your needs and to continually prune out the ones that don't prove useful. Once you have good sources coming to you on a regular basis, you can learn to quickly process and save relevant information for later.

For example, let's say that you subscribe to several e-mail newsletters about new technologies. There are apps that make it easy to process your inbox more quickly. One example is Newton[2] (by Cloud Magic). Available for Mac, iOS, and Android, it can bring all your e-mail accounts from different sources into one place, and make it easy to archive, delete, or save messages, by simple swipe gestures on your mobile devices. This makes it easy to process a large amount of e-mail more quickly than is possible using a typical desktop e-mail client.

There will continue to be innovation in ways to process information quickly—this is just one example. The idea is to find tools that help you move quickly through large amounts of information that are coming your way.

Saving and Bookmarking with Multiple Tools

You can also process and save information quickly by using an app that saves website articles for reading later. My favorite one is Pocket,[3] by Read It Later. You can find other useful apps for reading later in reviews like this one by Vicky Cassidy, "Beyond Bookmarks: The 10 Best Read It Later Apps for Saving Articles and Videos."[4] Pocket is my favorite for several reasons. You can install a widget or bookmarklet in your web browsers (desktop and mobile) that makes it easy to save an article with one click (removing ads and navigation). You can also add optional tags, making it easy to find all of your saved articles on specific topics later.

As I process my e-mail inbox, I often click on links to the most interesting articles from each newsletter, do a quick scan of each, and save in Pocket the ones I'm interested in. Later, I can go back and read them more in depth.

There is no need to have one tool for all of your saved sources. It's often easier to use different tools for different types of information. You could use Pocket for articles, Amazon wish lists for e-books, YouTube playlists for videos, and any tools that let you mark items as favorites.

There is also no need to save everything far into the future. Tools change over time, and over the years you may find yourself switching to newer tools. Many tools make it easy to export your lists, such as podcast apps— most of them make it easy to export a list of all of your podcasts for importing into a new app with an OPML file.

But often, by the time you're ready to migrate to a new tool, the information you've saved in the past is no longer very useful anyway. So you don't need to fear leaving it behind. There might be a period of overlap when you're transitioning to a new tool, but eventually all of your saved sources for a particular year or project will no longer be relevant. You can start a new year or a new project with a new tool.

When to Go Back and Read in Depth

I've heard people laugh about how they save lots of articles in a tool like Pocket and then never get around to going back and reading them. Yes, that happens! However, later in this book, I'll discuss some ideas for regularly going through your information, reading, evaluating, and learning more. For now, we're focusing on information gathering. In the next few sections, we'll look at ideas for the best places to get information from.

Newsletters, Feeds, and Groups

Some of the best technology news comes from e-mail newsletters, blog feeds, social media, and discussion groups.

Each of these types of sources has different advantages and disadvantages. Here are some suggestions.

A. E-mail Newsletters

Advantages: You're more likely to read them, since they arrive in your inbox.

Disadvantages: It's easy to feel overwhelmed, with too much e-mail to process.

Use these for: Topics you want to be updated on frequently.

You're more likely to at least glance at something that comes to your e-mail inbox, than sources that require you to remember to look at them. It can be overwhelming though, because you probably get too much e-mail for many different purposes already. One idea is to set up filters for all of your newsletters, and only process them as set times. I've abandoned that idea, because then it's the same problem of remembering to go look at them (in a filtered folder or mailbox).

Instead try using an e-mail app that allows you to quickly archive, delete, or forward each message.[5] Then use a triage approach, such as this: archive (so you can search for it later), delete (because you don't need to read this one today, but aren't ready to unsubscribe), or forward (to a read-later app, like Pocket or Evernote). Tools like Pocket and Evernote usually provide a private e-mail address for your account, so you can forward e-mail into it.[6] That is very useful.

Save the best newsletters to go through all at once. Click on the links to articles of interest and save those into Pocket or similar "read later" tools, then delete the newsletter.

These days, I never aim for "inbox zero" (a technique you may have heard of).[7] Instead, I think of my e-mail inbox as one long stream (like Twitter), and the entire e-mail box as a searchable database. It takes too much time to categorize messages into folders. Once you've pulled out important links or text into other apps, you can delete those messages and star or label ones that you might want to search for later—such as communications from coworkers about important tasks. These days, many workplaces use tools like Slack[8] instead of e-mail, which keeps many of those messages outside of your inbox. That makes your e-mail a more useful place to receive and process information from newsletters.

Below are some examples of e-mail newsletters that I find useful for keeping up with new technologies. Over time these will change of course, and if you're reading this a few years after this book was published, you'll want to find some new lists. Look for a list of best newsletters in the fields you care about, like this one, "35 Email Newsletters To Boost Your Career In Tech."[9]

You may find that for the newsletters you enjoy the most, you end up going to the sources that they use, and subscribing directly to them. That's fine, but not necessary unless you want more in-depth information on that topic. A good newsletter on topics you care about can save you a lot of time, by curating the best sources for you.

Remember to read newsletters from outside of your field, because creative ideas for libraries often come by combining ideas from other disciplines. Here are some newsletters that I find useful—all of them from outside the field of information science.

Austin Kleon
http://austinkleon.com/newsletter/
Austin Kleon is a writer and artist living in Austin, Texas. He often includes links to items about creativity that can be helpful when coming up with ideas for innovative library services.

Benedict Evans
http://ben-evans.com/newsletter/
Benedict Evans works at a venture capital firm that invests in technology companies. In his newsletter, he offers insightful analysis of new technologies in the world of mobile, virtual reality, internet-connected things, artificial intelligence, and search.

Brain Pickings, by Maria Popova
https://www.brainpickings.org/index.php/newsletter/
Maria Popova, a Bulgarian writer, blogger, and critic living in Brooklyn, New York, writes this wide-ranging topical newsletter on topics such as creativity, psychology, art, science, design, and philosophy. It can help you with ideas for creative thinking or productivity, and give you inspiration from thinkers in many fields.

Crypto-Gram, by Bruce Schneier
https://www.schneier.com/crypto-gram/
Bruce Schneier is a well-known expert on cryptography, security, and privacy and has been offering this newsletter since 1998. It's one of the

very best sources I know of for getting expert insight and analysis on what's happening in the world of cybersecurity.

Future Trends in Technology and Education, by Bryan Alexander
https://bryanalexander.org/future-trends-in-technology-and-education/
Bryan Alexander is a futurist, researcher, writer, speaker, consultant, and teacher. His monthly report focuses on how education is changing with the impact of digital technologies.

Good, by Good, a media brand and social impact company
https://www.good.is/newsletter
Good is an online and print magazine that focuses on ways to make things better and do good in the world. Their newsletter often contains stories of the impact of socially responsible companies and organizations, which can be inspiring as we think of how libraries can be integrated with community projects for social good.

Hacker Newsletter, by Hacker News
http://www.hackernewsletter.com
This newsletter from the popular website, Hacker News, focuses on the best articles about technology, programming, startup companies, and more.

Mobile Apps News, by Nicole Hennig
http://nicolehennig.com/mobile-apps-news/
This is my monthly newsletter that helps you stay current on the best mobile technologies. In addition to new apps and app updates, it covers emerging technologies, tips for using mobile effectively, and technology trends that impact libraries.

Product Hunt
https://www.producthunt.com/
Product Hunt is a website where users share and discover new products, such as apps, websites, books, or podcasts. It includes a voting system with comments, so people can "upvote" and discuss the products they are finding most useful. Subscribe to their tech digest[10] for daily e-mail updates. It's a good way to be the first to learn about new services and apps.

Quartz Daily Brief
http://qz.com/daily-brief/
The Quartz Daily Brief is mainly about politics and the economy, but also includes useful stories about new technologies in their "matters of debate" section. Quartz is a global business news publication, owned by Atlantic Media Company, publisher of *The Atlantic.*

TED: Ideas Worth Spreading
http://www.ted.com
TED is a nonprofit dedicated to spreading new ideas in the form of short, interesting presentations. It began in 1984 as a conference about technology, entertainment, and design (hence, the TED acronym). Now there are events around the world, known as TEDx events—independently run. Sign up for their e-mail alerts with daily or weekly options to get interesting technology news in the form of video presentations by experts.

Tidbits, by Adam and Tonya Engst
http://tidbits.com
Tidbits is a long-running newsletter about Apple products. If you use iPhones, iPads, a Mac, or any Apple product, this is a good way to keep up with the latest news.

UX Notebook, by Sarah Doody
http://www.theuxnotebook.com/
If you want to learn more about user experience design, subscribe to this newsletter by Sarah Doody, an expert UX designer.

B. Blog Feeds

Advantages: You can visit them when you want news about specific topics.

Disadvantages: You may forget to look at your feeds.

Use these for: Topics that you want to occasionally learn more about.

Many useful blogs these days have the option to subscribe via RSS or by e-mail. For those that you may want to look at only from time to time, subscribing to their RSS feeds can be useful. You can use a tool like Feedly,[11] or another RSS reader to search for a blog title, and subscribe to its updates. You can sort them into categories if you have a lot of feeds. Visit your feed reader once in a while to read the latest updates from your favorite blogs.

In addition to blogs from librarians, look for those from local organizations, universities, nonprofits, and so on—if they are of interest. Look also for blogs from particular people in your community that you wish to follow—students, professors, writers, and scholars. Look for blogs about technology, libraries, education, privacy, security, future trends, and technology ethics.

Here are a few that I find useful.

- Deeplinks—EFF: Electronic Frontier Foundation, https://www.eff.org/deeplinks. EFF covers issues related to security, privacy, and civil liberties online.

- Designing Better Libraries, http://dbl.lishost.org/blog. Steven Bell's blog focuses on user experience, design, and creativity in libraries.

- Evernote Blog, https://blog.evernote.com/. Evernote is very useful for taking notes in different formats. Their blog offers many useful tips and tricks.

- Fast Company, https://www.fastcompany.com/. Fast Company's blog offers many interesting stories about technology innovations.

- Hack Education, http://hackeducation.com/. Hack Education, by Audrey Watters, covers the history and future of educational technology.

- Mashable, http://mashable.com/category/tech/. The tech section of the news site Mashable is a good place to read about new technologies.

- The Next Web, http://thenextweb.com/. This is another technology news site with interesting stories about new and emerging technologies.

- Mind/Shift, https://ww2.kqed.org/mindshift/. Mind/Shift from KQED covers the latest in education news, with many stories about educational technologies.

- ProfHacker, http://www.chronicle.com/blogs/profhacker. ProfHacker from the Chronicle of Higher Education covers technology news as it relates to higher education.

- The Verge, http://www.theverge.com/tech. The tech section of the Verge covers the latest in new technologies.

C. Long-Form Writing Platforms

Advantages: The reading experience is clean and uncluttered, and many excellent writers publish here.

Disadvantages: There is so much good content that it's easy to become overwhelmed by your updates from these sources.

Use these for: Topics that you want to keep up with by reading "long-form" content. Use the e-mail updates for specific topics and writers that you want to hear from more frequently.

Another type of source worth getting information from are long-form writing platforms. Expect to see more of these in the future. For now, let's look at Medium as an example.

Medium

Medium is an alternative blogging platform, organized by topic instead of by author.[12] It was founded by Evan Williams and Biz Stone (the founders of Twitter). Unlike Twitter, writers are encouraged to write stories that are as long as they like.

The Medium writing tool is focused on clean, minimalistic design, with a lot of white space on every page. This makes it easy for readers to focus on the content, rather than clutter you see on many other sites.

Stories here are from both professional journalists and everyday people. When you find a story you like, you can bookmark it, and also recommend articles by clicking the "heart" after each story.

Authors can choose to give their work a Creative Commons license that facilitates open sharing.[13] Publishers can offer branded content with Medium, mapped to their own domain name, such as MondayNote[14] or Backchannel.[15]

Every story is tagged, and you can follow tags, authors, and publications. Updates come regularly to your e-mail with stories from sources you follow.

A few publications worth following on Medium are:

- Backchannel, https://backchannel.com. This publication is part of the Wired Media Group and features interesting technology analysis.
- Software Is Eating the World, https://medium.com/software-is-eating -the-world. Interesting technology news analysis from technology venture capital firm, a16z (Andreessen Horowitz).
- What's the Future of Work?, https://medium.com/the-wtf-economy. How work, business, and society face massive, technology-driven change. Curated by Tim O'Reilly, Steven Levy and Lauren Smiley.

I find Medium to be one of the richest sources of technology news of all the sources I currently follow. Once you've found topics, tags, and publications that are of interest, the daily e-mails are very focused on good information that is relevant to your specific interests.

D. Discussion Groups and Online Communities

Advantages: You can participate in communities of like-minded people, ask questions, and get advice.

Disadvantages: It's easy to spend hours following a comment thread that may not pay off for you. You may come across trolls and comment spam.

Use these for: Topics where you want to contribute to and follow discussions, ask questions, and become part of a virtual community.

Discussion groups have been around throughout Internet history and can be very useful. The platforms change over time, but if you find a community focused on your specific interests, the information shared there can often be quite valuable.

Here are some examples of communities I've found useful at the time of this writing. You will certainly find others in the future.

Google+ communities
Artificial Intelligence, https://plus.google.com/u/0/communities/116461000134682563789
A community for discussing developments in the field of artificial intelligence.

iPad Ed, https://plus.google.com/u/0/communities/117488594814613383470
A community for educators using iPads and other mobile devices in the classroom.

Mobile Devices, https://plus.google.com/u/0/communities/112915392661745517235
A community created by Guy Kawasaki for sharing news and tips about mobile devices on any platform.

Reddit
Education, https://www.reddit.com/r/education/
A community where educational stakeholders participate in thought-provoking discussions about educational policy, research, technology, and politics.

Futurology, https://www.reddit.com/r/Futurology/
This community is devoted to the field of future studies and evidence-based speculation about the development of humanity, technology, and civilization.

Libraries and Librarians, https://www.reddit.com/r/Libraries/
A community for discussion of a wide range of issues related to all types of libraries.

Technology, https://www.reddit.com/r/technology/
A community for discussing the latest developments in the world of technology.

Facebook groups
Design & UX for Libraries, https://www.facebook.com/groups/libux/

A group for discussing design and user experience for libraries, including the web, physical space, code, customer service—anything related to improving user experience in any type of library.

Library Entrepreneurship & Maker Services, https://www.facebook.com/groups/startup.library/
An official Member Initiative Group of the American Library Association. This group is focused on a creative, entrepreneurial approach to solving problems. Tools like design thinking, active learning, and lean startup help both makers and entrepreneurs, and can help libraries innovate internally.

MakerSpaces and the Participatory Library, https://www.facebook.com/groups/librarymaker/
A space for discussion about Makerspaces, digital media labs, and participatory/community spaces in libraries.

Wordpress and Librarians, https://www.facebook.com/groups/wordpress.librarians/
Use this group to ask and answer questions and to share information about using Wordpress for library websites.

Slack channels
LibUX, https://libraryux.slack.com
A place to discuss user experience in libraries.

E. Visual Sources from Social Media

Advantages: These tools are useful for sources where the visual information is important, such as photos, infographics, charts, and slide decks.

Disadvantages: It's easy to get lost in following your personal interests with these sources.

Use these for: Topics where visual information is primary.

Pinterest, https://www.pinterest.com
Use Pinterest for collecting visual information, such as infographics, step-by-step instructions, photos of library spaces, and so on. You can follow topic boards and individual people of interest.

Some examples that I find useful are as follows:

3D Printing, https://www.pinterest.com/jessdunnthis/3d-printing/
A board by designer Jessica Lea Dunn, a designer from Sydney, Australia. Follow to keep up with examples of what's possible with 3D printing.

Library Design Showcase, https://www.pinterest.com/amlibraries/library-design-showcase-2012/
American Libraries Magazine curates this board, which includes photos of newly designed spaces in libraries that feature technology.

Educational Technology, https://www.pinterest.com/cultofpedagogy/educational-technology/
A board about technology tools for use by teachers and students.

New Technology, https://www.pinterest.com/rickmsr2/new-technology/
A board about new technologies—mostly hardware and gadgets.

Internet of Things, https://www.pinterest.com/anujdwivedi89/internet-of-things/
Infographics and examples of the Internet of Things.

Slideshare
Use Slideshare to follow interesting people who create useful slide decks.[16] Often future trend reports will publish decks here. Once you find a useful deck, follow the person who created it, since they will usually post on topics you care about.

Here are a few examples of organizations or authors I follow—you may find these useful.

a16z, http://www.slideshare.net/a16z
Andreessen Horowitz is a Silicon Valley-based venture capital firm. They compile many useful reports and presentations about new and emerging technologies (see also their podcast listed in the chapter on multimedia resources).

Kleiner Perkins Caufield & Byers: Mary Meeker's Internet Trend Reports, http://www.slideshare.net/kleinerperkins
Mary Meeker's Internet Trend Report comes out annually and is a great way to learn about the latest technology trends. View her slide presentations for a quick overview with many interesting statistics (see also her listing in the section on trend reports).

Pew Research Center for Internet and American Life, http://www.slideshare.net/PewInternet
The Pew Research Center is well-known for its useful gathering of statistics, especially relating to how people use technologies. Looking at their slide decks is a useful way to scan their materials and keep up with their latest reports.

Sometimes slide decks and images are the best way to consume certain types of information. You can take in and understand information quickly and effectively when you see a well-designed chart, graph, or infographic. Keep an eye out for new social media tools like Pinterest and Slideshare that focus on the visual.

F. People and Organizations—Their Social Media Feeds

Advantages: These tools make it easy to follow particular people and groups with expertise on technologies.

Disadvantages: It can sometimes be challenging to separate out the technology-focused interests you have from everything else you follow on social media. It's also easy to find misinformation that people quickly share without reading or fact-checking.

Use these for: Getting current information and breaking news from particular individuals, groups, conferences, and organizations.

Social media tools like Twitter and Facebook are useful for following particular people and groups. Follow individual experts, libraries, non-profits, museums, schools, universities, and similar sources.

Twitter

One of the best ways to make Twitter more useful is to create lists and follow lists made by others.[17] That way you can easily separate out streams of topics you're interested in.

Twitter is also useful for following particular hashtags, such as those mentioned at conferences you attend.[18] Usually, these hashtag feeds have a short shelf-life, but they can be extremely useful during and right after conference sessions to get the latest information about specific topics and presentations.

A good way to follow your lists and hashtags is to use an app that allows you to view several different streams at once in a dashboard view. Good examples are Hootsuite[19] and Tweetdeck.[20] Apps like these usually have both mobile and desktop apps or can be accessed via their websites.

Use apps like Nuzzle[21] to easily follow top stories from your friends, and friends of friends. It sends out a daily e-mail of stories you may have missed that your contacts are tweeting about. That way it's easy to see important updates without needing to dip into the entire feed of people who you're following on Twitter.

Summary

There will always be new tools like these being created. Find and use the best of them to keep up with sources of information on new and emerging technologies.

Take advantage of tools, features, and apps that allow you to organize and filter your information, so you can quickly see just the topics and people you wish to follow. Look for ways to automate your flow of information, which is something I'll discuss in the section on dealing with information overload.

Multimedia Resources: Video, Audio, and Courses

Some of the best technology information is available from audio and video sources. Here are some tips for finding and using them.

A. Video Sites

YouTube, Vimeo, and similar sites are good places to find information on emerging technologies. On these sites, you can find channels, people, and organizations to follow. Look for conferences, educational organizations, publishers of technology books, and similar channels.

Video is of course good for learning specific skills, but for keeping up with new technologies, often you need to learn about topics at a higher level—concepts, future trends, and so on. Video sites are useful for that because they offer conference talks and lectures. Within sites like YouTube and Vimeo, you can make your own playlists on different topics, and keep a "watch later" playlist.

The following channels are good to follow for keeping up with new technologies.

Future trends forum, Bryan Alexander, https://www.youtube.com/playlist?list=PLlcx8yl6hlPC3QjlbIHzxGqCP3qRa0zcg
Bryan Alexander is a futurist, writer, and speaker working on how technology transforms education. This playlist is made up of interviews with experts on future trends in educational technologies. His e-mail newsletter was mentioned in the previous section.[22]

GEL: Good Experience Live, https://vimeo.com/gelconference
These are the videos from an excellent conference called "GEL," which stands for "Good Experience Live." It explores good user experience in

many different settings and is held each spring in New York.[23] See the conferences chapter for more about this event.

Ignite: A Series of Speedy Presentations, http://www.ignitetalks.io/
Ignite events are held in cities around the world. With the Ignite format, presenters get only 20 slides in which to do their talk. The slides automatically advance every 15 seconds. This keeps the talks fast, fun, and informative. Look for science- and technology-related playlists within the site, such as http://www.ignitetalks.io/playlists/cool -science-talks.

MIT CSAIL, https://www.youtube.com/user/MITCSAIL
If you are familiar with particular departments at universities that are doing interesting research, look for their YouTube channels. MIT's CSAIL is the Computer Science & Artificial Intelligence Laboratory at MIT, where a lot of cutting edge research happens.

MIT Media Lab, https://www.youtube.com/user/mitmedialab
MIT's Media Lab is another site with interesting videos on new technologies. Look to your local universities and higher education departments for video channels as well.

O'Reilly Publishers, https://www.youtube.com/channel/UC3BGlwmI -Vk6PWyMt15dKGw
O'Reilly Publishers are well-known for their many books on new technologies. Their YouTube channel includes interesting talks by experts who speak at their conferences. It's a great way to learn something from conferences you weren't able to attend in person.

Pecha Kucha: 20 images, 20 seconds, http://www.pechakucha.org/
Pecha Kucha is a format for giving short presentations, similar to Ignite. This video channel includes short presentations given around the world in this concise format (20 slides, 20 seconds each). See this presentation for an example about making presentations, http://www.pechakucha.org/ presentations/how-to-create-slides. Not all videos here are about specific technologies, but you can use the site search to find those. Here's an example of a technology topic—this one is about 3D printing for human body parts, http://www.pechakucha.org/presentations/printing-the-human-body.

PopTech—Technology Talks, http://www.poptech.org/blog/tagged/24
PopTech brings together innovators from fields such as science, technology, design, ecological innovation, and more. At their events, participants share provocative questions and new ideas with their peers. Videos from these events are fun to watch. They are grouped into categories such as technology (http://www.poptech.org/blog/categories/Technology),

education (http://www.poptech.org/blog/categories/Education), or science (http://www.poptech.org/blog/categories/Science).

SXSW, https://www.youtube.com/channel/
UC2YKXCQ8wt1RFpQEELwILCQ
South by Southwest holds an amazing and huge conference each year in Austin, Texas. See video presentations from their Interactive conference in playlists like this one, https://www.youtube.com/playlist?list=PLXs_3rGeYdImeBCUswTffczBaeAODWWQE. Their Education conference is also worth following, https://www.youtube.com/user/SXSWEDU.

Talks at Google, https://www.youtube.com/channel/
UCbmNph6atAoGfqLoCL_duAg
Google hosts many interesting talks, with experts speaking on a wide range of topics. See their technology playlist to focus on new technologies, https://www.youtube.com/playlist?list=PLGGpady h0wS7XnpWK8ofxWhL7F72KcDRj.

TED Talks, https://www.ted.com/talks
TEDTalks is a well-known series of interesting presentations on topics in the fields of technology, entertainment, and design, or "TED." On their website, you can filter the videos by topics, such as technology (https://www.ted.com/talks?sort=newest&topics%5B%5D=Technology) or science (https://www.ted.com/talks?sort=newest&topics%5B%5D =Technology&topics%5B%5D=Science). Use the handy sort widget to find videos by duration, such as 0–6 minutes, 6–12 minutes, 12–18 minutes, and so on. This is handy if you only have a few minutes to watch something. Another widget makes it easy to sort by characteristics such as, "jaw-dropping," "funny," "persuasive," or "inspiring." There is a wealth of content here. You may also want to subscribe to their YouTube channel, https://www.youtube.com/user/TEDtalksDirector.

TWIT: This Week in Tech, https://twit.tv/shows/this-week-in-tech
This Week in Tech is a video podcast hosted by Leo Laporte. Each week in a new episode, he discusses current issues in technology and society. It's a good way to keep up with what's new each week.

B. iTunes U, MOOCs, and Online Course Platforms

iTunes U publishes a large amount of excellent content from universities, nonprofits, museums, and other organizations.[24] You may not have time to watch the video lectures of an entire course, but often there are particular lectures worth watching. Professors sometimes make their iTunes U courses available exclusively to their own students (with enroll codes or special links), but there is still a very large amount of free content open for anyone to view, since that was the original mission of iTunes U—to bring educational content to the world.

You can view iTunes U content on desktop or laptop computers using iTunes software, available for Mac or Windows.[25] On your mobile devices, you can use iTunes U[26] for iOS or Tunesviewer[27] for Android and Linux.

Here are two examples.

"Entrepreneurial Thought Leaders" by Stanford eCorner, https://itunes.apple.com/us/itunes-u/entrepreneurial-thought-leaders/id384233886?mt=10 This is a seminar series at Stanford University on entrepreneurship. Hear from top experts on timely technology topics.

"The Power of Connectivity," from the Aspen Ideas Festival, https://itunes.apple.com/us/itunes-u/the-power-of-connectivity/id1141986317?mt=10 This is an interesting set of audio and video talks from the Aspen Ideas Festival. It includes topics such as "Who should safeguard our data?," "Closing the digital divide," and "On the road to artificial intelligence."

Massive Open Online Courses (MOOCs) and other online courses are another good way to find excellent video content. MOOCs are useful because even though you may not find time to participate in an entire course, you can still skim courses and watch individual lectures (since MOOCs are free). You can also look for reading lists from courses on new technologies. The major MOOC platforms are Coursera, edX, and Udacity.[28]

Here are some examples.

Awareness-Based Systems Change with u.lab—How to Sense and Actualize the Future—MIT, https://www.edx.org/course/awareness-based-systems-change-u-lab-how-mitx-15-671-0x#!

Design Thinking for Innovation—University of Virginia, https://www.coursera.org/learn/design-thinking-innovation

Educational Technology—Georgia Tech, https://www.udacity.com/course/educational-technology—ud915

Innovation Management—Erasmus University Rotterdam, https://www.coursera.org/learn/innovation-management

Multimodal Literacies: Communication and Learning in the Era of Digital Media—University of Illinois at Urbana-Champaign, https://www.coursera.org/learn/multimodal-literacies

Responsible Innovation: Ethics, Safety and Technology—Delft University of Technology, https://www.edx.org/course/responsible-innovation-ethics-safety-delftx-ri101x

u.lab: Leading From the Emerging Future—MIT, https://www.edx.org/course/u-lab-leading-emerging-future-mitx-15-671-1x#!

These particular courses may not be available at the time you are reading this, but it's easy to search each of these platforms to find courses on topics of interest.

Lynda.com

Another good site to use for technology training is Lynda.com.[29] Their courses are usually focused on step-by-step instructions for learning a particular tool or app, so most of those are better for later stages in your process when you are implementing a new technology. They can also be useful for your own personal development—to learn coding or web design skills. Many universities have institutional subscriptions to *Lynda.com*, so if you work at one, you might be able to take advantage of this. If not, personal subscriptions are available for a low monthly fee, with a free trial available.[30]

But, for emerging technology exploration, there are some useful courses. One topic we'll discuss later in this book is a process called "design thinking." There are several courses on *Lynda.com* about this topic, such as "Design Thinking: Understanding the Process," https://www.lynda.com/Interaction-Design-tutorials/Design-Thinking-Understanding-Process/476938-2.html.

You can also learn about accessibility, with several courses available at https://www.lynda.com/Accessibility-training-tutorials/1286-0.html. Other useful courses can be found in the categories of instructional design, https://www.lynda.com/Instructional-Design-training-tutorials/1796-0.html, and user experience design, https://www.lynda.com/guides/user-experience/career-in-user-experience. If you're an emerging technologies librarian, you'll often be asked to implement training for your staff or users, so these are good skills to have.

C. Podcasts: Digital Audio Programming

Listening to audio podcasts can be a fun and useful way to learn about new technologies. There are many excellent programs on technology topics. It can be convenient to listen to these while exercising, doing routine chores, or during your commute.

Listen to podcasts using mobile apps like Pocket Casts[31] (iOS and Android), Overcast[32] (iOS), and many others.[33] On desktops and laptops, you can listen using iTunes for Mac or Windows, or via websites like Stitcher Radio.[34] Most podcasts are also available on the websites of the podcast producer.

Here are some recommended podcasts for keeping up with new technologies.

A16z (Andreessen Horowitz), http://a16z.com/podcasts/
A very interesting show that features industry experts discussing the latest developments in technology and culture. Produced by Andreessen Horowitz, a Silicon Valley-based venture capital firm.

Anatomy of Next: Utopia (Founders Fund), http://foundersfund.com/anatomy-of-next/podcasts/
In Anatomy of Next, they challenge dystopian ideas about new technologies and present an optimistic view of the future.

AppleVis (*AppleVis.com*), http://www.applevis.com/podcasts
This show is for blind and low-vision users of Apple technology. They feature demos and walk-throughs of apps, along with tips for using Apple devices securely.

Canvas (Relay FM), https://www.relay.fm/canvas
This podcast is about mobile productivity. Hosted by Federico Viticci and Fraser Speirs, it covers the best apps for iPhone and iPad.

Click (BBC World Service), http://www.bbc.co.uk/programmes/p002w6r2
This interesting program from the BBC covers technology news from around the world. It's useful for getting an international perspective.

Exponent (Ben Thompson and James Allworth), http://exponent.fm/
This podcast focuses on how technology is affecting society. It's hosted by Ben Thompson and James Allworth. Thompson also writes an excellent blog about the business and strategy of technology, see *Stratechery.com*.

Flash Forward (Rose Eveleth), http://www.flashforwardpod.com/
This show imagines a different possible future scenario in each episode. Scenarios such as: a future where presidential candidates have thousands of Tweets and Tumblr posts and Instagrams in their online record or a

future where instead of traditional schools, everybody learns on their own time, on tablets and guided by artificial intelligence.

Futuropolis (Popular Science), http://www.popsci.com/authors/futuropolis
By talking with scientists, engineers, and innovators, this show explores everyday life in the future. They cover topics like 3-D movies, total recall of everyone's life events, the future of robots, and more.

Future Tense (Australian Broadcasting Company), http://www.abc.net.au/radionational/programs/futuretense/
The Australian Broadcasting Company produces this interesting podcast on the social and cultural changes that come with new technologies. Episodes include topics like digital security, human microchipping, and the future of handwriting.

Note to Self (WNYC Studios), http://www.wnyc.org/shows/notetoself/
Manoush Zomorodi hosts this interesting podcast about preserving our humanity in the digital age. Some topics she discusses include Silicon Valley's diversity problem, "echo chambers" in democracy, and looking at what kinds of information Facebook has about you.

Pessimist's Archive (Louis Anslow), https://soundcloud.com/pessimistsarc
To counter fears of new technologies, it's helpful to look at history. This podcast looks back in time at stories of how people got worried about new technologies that we now take for granted. The first episode focuses on the Sony Walkman and fears about what would happen when everyone had one.

Recode Decode (Vox Media), http://www.recode.net/podcasts
Hosted by prominent technology journalist Kara Swisher, this podcast is made up of interviews with business leaders and media personalities who are outspoken about new technologies. Some topics include how machine learning will be part of every doctor's job in the future, how to fix the diversity problem in technology hiring, and what to do about the future threat of artificial intelligence taking jobs.

Stuff from the Future (*HowStuffWorks.com*), http://shows.howstuffworks.com/stuff-from-the-future-podcast.htm
The staff of HowStuffWorks explores technology issues of the future, such as nanotechnology leading to a cure for cancer, the future of air travel, the future of the user interface, and the future of privacy.

Tech Tent (BBC World Service), http://www.bbc.co.uk/programmes/p01plr2p/episodes/downloads

This BBC show covers current technology news with episodes on topics such as big data and fake news. It covers what's happening in Europe and around the world.

TEDTalks Technology (TEDTalks), https://itunes.apple.com/gb/podcast/tedtalks-technology/id470624027?mt=2
TEDTalks are well-known interesting presentations on topics in the fields of technology, entertainment, and design, or "TED." Use this link to subscribe to just the technology-focused topics. Some interesting episodes include, "Your smartphone is a civil rights issue," "Machine intelligence makes human morals more important," and "How computers are learning to be creative."[35]

What's Tech (The Verge), https://art19.com/shows/whats-tech
In this podcast, experts explain specific technologies in brief, clear, enjoyable ways that are easy to understand. Some episodes include, "Why smartphone batteries explode, and why they may get worse," "How HTTPS is slowly but surely making the Internet safer," and "What you need to know about doxxing, the average internet user's nightmare."[36]

Wonderland: On the Creative Power of Play (How We Get to Next with Steven Johnson), https://howwegettonext.com/wonderland-podcast-dc6e08ab07f6#.3ru8glh1u
Inspired by Steven Johnson's book, *Wonderland: How Play Made The Modern World,*[37] this podcast includes conversations about creativity and invention. Hosted by the author, it's about play and innovation, and includes interviews with leading scientists, musicians, and programmers.

Discovery tools for podcasts
To find new podcasts on technology topics, here are some useful tools.

Audiosear.ch, https://www.audiosear.ch/
Audiosear.ch is a full text search and recommendation tool for podcasts and digital audio. Their service converts speech into text, and then indexes it to create a searchable database. One way to use it is to search for your favorite authors of books on new technologies, since you can often find them being interviewed discussing their new books. Use their alerts page to set up searches for the authors and books you are interested in, https://www.audiosear.ch/alerts.

Podcat, https://www.podcat.com
Search for specific people who are mentioned or interviewed in podcasts. For example, search for the author "Kevin Kelly," and find a list of podcast episodes that mention him.

Product Hunt, https://www.producthunt.com/podcasts

Product Hunt is a popular community where enthusiasts share information about the best apps, websites, hardware projects, and more. The podcasts section recommends specific episodes each day, and most are technology-related.

To learn more about the best podcasts and how to find them, see my report, *Podcast Literacy: Recommending the Best Educational, Diverse, and Accessible Podcasts for Library Users,* published as part of the Library Technology Reports series from the American Library Association.[38]

D. Apps That Read Out Loud to You

Another way to get your technology news in audio format is to use an app such as Capti Voice Narrator that turns text into speech.[39] This app is free and available for iPhone, iPad, Windows, and Mac[40], as well as web browsers such as Chrome, Firefox, and Safari. You can select from a number of different voices, select a speed in words per minute, and use a browser bookmarklet to save stories from web pages into a playlist that you can listen to later. You can also pull in content from services like Dropbox, Google Drive, Pocket, and Project Gutenberg. It can read EPUB, Word, Daisy, HTML, PDF, and other formats. It's especially useful for people who have vision impairments, dyslexia, or other disabilities. There are video tutorials available to see how it works.[41]

This has some of the same advantages as podcasts do, such as being able to listen to your readings while doing routine chores, exercising, or during commutes. The voices sound computer-generated, but they do a much better job than early versions of this type of technology—they really aren't hard to listen to—and speech technology is always improving.

Summary

Using multimedia resources can save you time, especially with audio programs that you can listen to while doing routine tasks. Sometimes a topic that you will read about in an article will have a more in-depth explanation in a podcast where it's being discussed. Podcasts are especially good for discussions of the ethics and social effects of new technologies. Courses, or parts of courses, can also be useful as a way to get a more in-depth understanding of a particular new technology.

Keep in mind that in this report I'm not talking about the typical "how-to" videos about hardware or software that you often find on YouTube (though those are handy). Instead I'm recommending sources that will help you see trends and understand the big picture and social implications of new technologies.

Conferences and Local Events

Conferences and local events are a great way to learn about new technologies, discuss issues with others, and get inspired. When you are deciding which conferences to attend, consider choosing something other than your usual professional associations. You can bring innovative new ideas into the world of libraries from other fields.

Here are some ideas for conferences I've attended over the years that were very helpful in bringing new ideas to the MIT Libraries. Most of these are very interdisciplinary and attract people from a variety of fields. When you hear excellent talks about methods of innovation, creativity, or user experience from other fields, it can inspire you with ideas for your library.

Conferences: Outside the Library Profession

Instead of going to the same events year after year, try some new ones outside of your field, like these.

GEL: Good Experience Live, http://creativegood.com/gel/
This event happens for a few days each spring in New York City. It's a gathering of experience leaders from many different fields, giving inspiring talks about how they have created a good experience for their users. It also includes a day of experiential training in small groups where you go on mini-field trips in different parts of the city.

SXSW: South by Southwest Conference, https://www.sxsw.com/conference/ and SXSW edu, http://sxswedu.com/
This well-known conference focuses on what's coming up in the world of technology, culture, and entertainment. It's where startups often announce innovative new services and technologies. It happens in Austin, Texas every year. The SXSW edu event focuses on what's new in educational technologies for all types of education. Both of these conferences are full of good information about emerging technologies.

UI 21: User Interface (Jared Spool), https://ui21.uie.com/
This conference happens annually in the Boston area. It's a great way to learn the latest techniques for user interface design and user experience. The format is useful because it features two full days where you choose one of the concurrent hands-on workshops (which lasts all day).

In between those two days is a more traditional event format where you hear a series of excellent talks by user experience experts.

IA Summit (Information Architecture), http://www.iasummit.org/
This annual conference, sponsored by the American Society for Information Science and Technology (ASIS&T), is for learning about user experience design, information architecture, and all types of content management that is focused on users. It is an excellent event and brings together people from many fields who want to learn about user experience design.

O'Reilly Design Conference, http://conferences.oreilly.com/design/ux-interaction-iot-us
This is another very interdisciplinary event with user researchers, user experience designers, product managers, and entrepreneurs sharing best practices in these fields. It's very user-focused and is held in San Francisco.

Conferences: Inside the Library Profession

I'm sure you are familiar with conferences within the library profession. Here are a few of those conferences that are especially good for learning about new technologies.

Code4Lib, https://code4lib.org/conference
This participatory event is for people who write code and work in libraries, but you don't have to be a coder yourself to get a lot out of this event. You will be sure to hear about many innovative projects that are being done in libraries everywhere. It's held in a different U.S. city every year. Here's how Code4Lib describes itself: "code4lib isn't entirely about code or libraries. It is a volunteer-driven collective of hackers, designers, architects, curators, catalogers, artists and instigators from around the world, who largely work for and with libraries, archives, and museums on technology 'stuff.'"[42]

Internet Librarian, http://internet-librarian.infotoday.com
This conference happens every year in Monterey, California and brings together librarians who are presenting about all sorts of innovative services and technologies in their libraries. It's a great way to network with your peers and hear about the latest technologies being implemented in libraries. I've presented at this conference several times over the years and enjoyed networking with colleagues in the beautiful location of Monterey.

LITA Forum, http://forum.lita.org/
This is a 3-day event held annually in different parts of the United States. It's another excellent way to learn about the latest developments in

technologies that libraries are using in their services and a good place to network with colleagues.

Searching for New Events

A good place to search for new conference ideas is the website and app, Lanyrd, http://lanyrd.com/. Within the site you can browse conferences and events by topic, such as educational technology, library technology, and user experience. You can subscribe to get e-mail updates on conferences you might be interested in.

Virtual Events

If you don't have a budget for attending conferences, try virtual events, such as webinars, online summits, and the like. They are good ways to keep up without spending money on travel.

These events are offered by regional library associations, library schools, and many other businesses and organizations. Sometimes they are a one-hour introduction to a topic, and other times they are a gathering that lasts a day or two, with several speakers on related topics. Some are free, some have a fee, and the fees are usually reasonable.

If you sign up and don't have time to watch the event video live, most events will send you a recording that you can watch later when it's convenient. It's useful to do these events live though, because they usually include a text-based question and answer session via chat in the webinar software (WebEX, Adobe Connect, Go to Meeting, or Google Hangouts).

Here are a few examples.

Online mini-conference: Library 2.016: Libraries of the Future: School of Information at San José State University—free
http://www.library20.com/future

O'Reilly Media webcasts—free
http://www.oreilly.com/webcasts/

User Research for Everyone: a one-day virtual conference, Rosenfeld Media
http://www.userresearchforeveryone.com/

WebJunction
http://learn.webjunction.org/

23 Things
http://www.heleneblowers.info/2012/08/6-years-of-23-things.html

23 Things was a learning project created by Helene Blowers in 2006. She created the project as a way to encourage librarians to learn and adapt to new technologies. The format involves several weeks of hands-on learning, with participants discussing everything with a network of peers and colleagues.

This format is a very popular and effective way to offer training on new technologies, and many groups from around the world have used it. For an example, see 23 Mobile Things—NEFLIN, http://neflin23 mobilethings.blogspot.com/. Look for future events in this popular format.

Keep an eye out for online events and get on the e-mail lists of the organizations who offer events of interest to you.

Local Events

Often, depending on where you live, there are local events of interest. In addition to your usual professional organization's local events, look for those outside of your field, on related topics.

One of the best places to look is on *Meetup.com*. Many interesting technology groups use Meetup to organize and promote their meetings.

In the Boston area, I've attended meet-ups such as the following:

Boston VR: Virtual Reality
http://www.meetup.com/Boston-Virtual-Reality/
This is an example of a meet-up that brings in experts to offer presentations and demos of the latest technologies related to virtual reality.

Boston AR: Augmented/Mixed Reality
http://www.meetup.com/BostonAR/
This is another example of a meet-up that brings in experts to offer presentations and demos, this one about augmented and mixed reality.

New England Chapter of ASIS&T
http://www.meetup.com/neasist/
Local chapters of your professional associations such as this one usually offer events that help you keep up with the latest technologies.

Enter your zip code on *Meetup.com* and browse the technology section to find many interesting events and clubs. Look for those that meet on a regular basis with a significant number of people. If you are in a location near a university, there will often be interesting events organized by science or technology experts from those universities.

Unconferences, BarCamps, PodCamps

An unconference is a meeting that is organized from the bottom up by its participants.[43] There are a wide range of events that use this model and they use different names, such as BarCamp or THATCamp.

Usually, the agenda is created by the attendees at the beginning of the meeting. Anyone who wants to initiate a topic can claim a time and space. The price of attendance is usually either free or very low. This type of conference works well when the people attending have a high degree of knowledge and want a way to share expertise and discuss ideas.

When podcasting was new, there were Podcamps, with many well-known podcasters sharing ideas. Anyone could attend, listen, ask questions, and learn from the experts. These days Podcamps are still being created and they cover all forms of new media, such as blogging, podcasting, video, and more.[44]

For tips and advice on attending these types of events, see "unConferencing – how to prepare to attend an unconference," by Kaliya Hamlin from unconference.net.[45]

Events at Local Colleges and Universities

Be sure to look for events at your local universities—often there are free lectures that you can attend to learn about cutting edge technologies. Get on the e-mail lists for the departments that offer topics of interest. If you work at a university library, it's easy to attend events at your own university.

Trend Reports

Another type of publication worth following is the trend report. Some of these are expensive, but you don't need to purchase them to get the best information. You can usually find summaries and slide presentations of the expensive ones, and many reports are available for free.

Of course, no one knows the future, and these may or may not be correct. But when you regularly read reports from different sources, you start to see certain themes emerging.

Here are a few examples of reports that are worth following, and there will likely be new ones in the future. You can search the phrase "trend report" along with relevant terms, such as "educational technology trend report."

Examples

Mary Meeker's Internet Trends Report, http://www.kpcb.com/internet-trends

Mary Meeker, a venture capitalist and former Wall Street securities analyst, produces one of the most famous and detailed Internet trend reports every year. You can find her slides online after each yearly presentation. You can also find many articles in the technology press focusing on specific aspects of her talk.

LITA top tech trends, http://www.ala.org/lita/about/committees/lit-ttt

ALA's LITA sponsors a technology trends committee every year. You can find the results of their panel discussion on their website and in American Libraries Magazine.[46]

Trends from the Center for the Future of Libraries, American Library Association,
http://www.ala.org/transforminglibraries/future/trends

These trend reports from the Center for the Future of Libraries are available in seven categories: society, technology, education, the environment, politics and government, economics, and demographics. Each trend section discusses how those trends are developing and why it matters.

NMC (New Media Consortium) Horizon Report, http://www.nmc.org/publication-type/horizon-report/

NMC publishes several trend report editions each year: K-12, museums, higher education, and library. They cover trends, challenges, and developments in technology for each area they cover.

PSFK Trend Reports, http://www.psfk.com/reports

PSFK is a firm that offers trend reports and consulting to businesses. Their reports are on a wide range of trends, including the future of work, virtual reality, future of health, and more. Prices range from free to $750 for each report, but you can find free summary slide decks on Slideshare, http://www.slideshare.net/psfk. See some free briefings here: http://www.psfk.com/reports. Though these might seem out of scope because they are aimed at businesses, they are useful because they give you ideas about trends in the larger context of society. Their blog includes posts organized by demographic, such as Baby Boomer, Children, Gen Z, LGBT, Infants, and Millennials.[47]

TrendWatching, http://trendwatching.com
TrendWatching is a firm that offers reports, conferences, and consulting on trends to businesses. In addition to their paid services, they have a free series of trend briefings, http://trendwatching.com/freepublications/. These are consumer trends, but are useful for understanding social trends in general and can spark ideas for innovative library services. See this report on consumer trends, for an example, "5 Consumer Trends for 2016," http://trendwatching.com/trends/5-trends-for-2016/.

Pew Research Center: Internet, Science and Tech, http:// www.pewinternet.org/
Pew Research Center is a nonpartisan group that conducts research about the issues and trends shaping our society. They are known for their data-driven social science research and their many useful statistics and reports.

You can subscribe to their monthly newsletter and report alerts. Some recent topics include libraries and learning, book reading, and digital readiness. See their presentations page for useful summaries of recent data, http://www.pewinternet.org/category/presentations/.

Gartner's Hype Cycle for Emerging Technologies, http:// www.gartner.com/technology/research/methodologies/hype-cycle.jsp
Gartner Research is known for their "hype cycle" which represents the cycle of maturity and adoption of specific technologies. If you don't have institutional access to this expensive report, you can still find plenty of information in the press by searching for articles that mention it.[48]

You may have heard of their hype cycles, which include the following terms describing the stages a new technology goes through before becoming mainstream.[49]

- Technology trigger
- Peak of inflated expectations
- Trough of disillusionment
- Slope of enlightenment
- Plateau of productivity

See this site for full explanations, Gartner Hype Cycle, http://www.gartner .com/technology/research/methodologies/hype-cycle.jsp. Look for a press release each year that summarizes the report, like this one: "2016 Hype Cycle for Emerging Technologies Identifies Three Key Trends That

Organizations Must Track to Gain Competitive Advantage," http://www.gartner.com/newsroom/id/3412017.

MIT Technology Review: 10 Breakthrough Technologies, https://www.technologyreview.com/lists/technologies/2016/
Every year Technology Review publishes "10 Breakthrough Technologies." These technologies cover many areas, from "power from the air" to "robots that teach each other." This is a good list to watch for each year, with an article for each technology that helps you understand the trend. They also sponsor an annual event about emerging technologies called EmTech at MIT.[50] Look for the videos online if you can't attend.

Harvard Business Review: 8 Tech Trends to Watch in 2016, https://hbr.org/2015/12/8-tech-trends-to-watch-in-2016
Harvard Business Review publishes a trend list every year that is worth reading.

Books

You might wonder how you could find time to read a whole book about a new technology while being bombarded with information. The answer is—you don't usually need to. Skimming and scanning, as described in an earlier section, is what you want to do at this stage.

If you do come across a book that is perfectly interesting and relevant, you can eventually read the whole thing. But often you can get what you need from scanning. Luckily, it's easy to do that these days. Here are some ideas.

Download Free Samples of E-Books

Just about every online store or publisher these days offers free samples of their e-books. Between scanning the table of contents and reading the sample, often you can get what you need to know without buying the book.

The Amazon Kindle app[51] is easy to install on your mobile devices, so you can read your e-book samples in spare moments, such as in waiting rooms or on public transportation. In the Kindle app, you can sort your e-books into collections and name them what you like, so I always keep a collection called "samples" and put all my samples there for easy access when I have time. You can set aside regular times to read your samples and from there decide which books you might want to buy or borrow to read. You can save notes from just the samples if that is enough. Google Play Books and iBooks are similar apps that work in the same way, with e-books from Google or Apple.

Store PDF and EPUB Books in the Cloud and in a Mobile App

Often you will find that publishers of technology books make free or paid e-books available as PDFs or EPUB files that you get directly from their websites.[52] Keep them in one place in your cloud apps (like Dropbox), and then easily import them into one mobile app on your devices—I use iBooks for this. When you import PDFs from Dropbox to iBooks on your iPhone or iPad, it recognizes the format and puts them into a collection called PDFs. That way you always know where they are and can read them in spare moments.

I have a Dropbox folder called "to read," and in it a folder for each year. At the beginning of each new calendar year, I make a new folder and put all my new PDF and EPUB books into it, so I can easily access them from my laptop, iPhone, or iPad.

Browse New Books in Bookstores and Libraries

Whenever you are in good bookstores and libraries, be sure to browse the technology sections for topics you are following. These days it's easy to snap a quick photo of the cover with your smartphone, or scan the barcode using shopping apps like Amazon or Pic2Shop[53] (which connects to Worldcat to find local libraries with the book). Later you can download the free samples to read and decide which ones to buy. You can support independent bookstores by buying directly from them.

Be sure to visit some of the best bookstores when you are visiting other cities or universities. For example, in the Boston area, visit The MIT Press Bookstore (https://mitpress.mit.edu/books/bookstore), in Seattle visit Ada's Technical Books and Cafe (http://www.seattletechnicalbooks.com/) and The Elliot Bay Book Company (http://www.elliottbaybook.com/), and in Portland, Oregon visit Powell's Bookstore (http://www.powells.com/). Look for large independent bookstores, stores that specialize in technology books, and university bookstores.

Often these stores will have staff members who are very good at curating collections on technology topics that you are interested in. I often find books this way that I wouldn't have heard about from other sources.

Listen to Interviews of the Authors of Technology Books on Podcast Episodes

If you've heard of an interesting technology title, but haven't had time to read it, you can often learn a lot by listening to interviews of the author on various podcasts. To find these interviews, use a search engine to search for the author's name with the words, "podcast" and "interview." For a more specific search than Google provides, with the possibility to set up alerts, try *Audiosear.ch* (https://www.audiosear.ch/). This tool is a full-text search engine for podcasts and radio. They transform speech into text, and analyze and index it to create their database. Use their alerts page to set up searches for the authors and books you are interested in: https://www.audiosear.ch/alerts. You'll receive an e-mail when your author is interviewed on a podcast. You might also find author interviews and speeches on YouTube.

Use Apps and Websites That Summarize Books

You might scoff at the idea of reading only summaries, but some people find these helpful and get enough out of them to decide whether to go deeper. There are apps that create summaries of nonfiction titles for you. One example is Blinkist (https://www.blinkist.com/), a subscription service that creates 2-minute reads based on key messages of each book. You can choose to receive text or audio and review the main concepts of a book in 15 minutes. They cover topics such as science, entrepreneurship, and communication. For a free site (but with fewer titles), try Actionable Books, http://www.actionablebooks.com/. They summarize and highlight key concepts from important business books. Another useful site with book summaries is Deconstructing Excellence, http://www.deconstructing excellence.com/, which covers books related to the topic of how to be a top performer in any field.

Read for Speed, Make Book Reading a Priority, and Other Tips

Speed reading apps are another tool you might find useful. These apps use a variety of techniques for helping you read faster, such as "rapid serial visual presentation," which involves displaying single words in rapid succession on your screen. I enjoy using an iOS app called Accelerator, http://acceleratorapp.com/, which flashes one word at a time on the screen (you can adjust this in settings for 2–4 words at a time). You can experiment with changing the speed until you can read faster and faster. It easily connects to services like Pocket and Instapaper where you saved articles you want to read. A similar app for Android that gets good reviews is called A Faster Reader, http://downloads.tomsguide.com/A-Faster-Reader,0301-54896.html.

For more ideas on how to read faster, make reading books a priority, and how to get more out of your reading, see "Warren Buffett's Best Kept Secret to Success: The Art of Reading, Remembering, and Retaining More Books," https://open.buffer.com/how-to-read-more-and-remember-it-all/.

Popular Culture and Science Fiction

It's likely that you are interacting with popular culture and science fiction from time to time—by reading books, watching TV shows and movies, reading comic books or graphic novels, and playing games. All of these sources are potentially useful for your project of keeping up with emerging technologies.

Technological Impacts on Society and Ethical Concerns of New Technologies

Studying popular culture helps you understand the underlying assumptions of society—aspects of culture that are easy to take for granted. According to entrepreneur Rachel Wayne, "Studying pop culture reveals the underlying assumptions, power structures, and philosophical and moral constructs of the society that produces those cultural products."[54] Depictions of technology use by fictional characters bring to mind both utopian visions and dystopian fears that we all have about new technologies. Fictional scenarios can be a good way to explore ethical ideas about the uses of technology.

Science fiction is especially useful for thinking about solutions to the ethical problems of new technologies. Works of science fiction can influence scientists and engineers who are working on new technologies. According to Patrick Purdy in UX Magazine, "Gene Roddenberry could never have imagined that a prop from his TV show would change the world, but that's exactly what happened when he introduced the communicator on the first episode of *Star Trek* in 1966. Just six short years later, in 1973, Martin Cooper made the first public cell phone call from a handheld device. Afterward he acknowledged that *Star Trek* had inspired him to develop the technology."[55]

Robert Sawyer, writing about the purpose of science fiction, says, "At the core of science fiction is the notion of extrapolation—of asking, 'If this goes on, where will it lead?' . . . our job is not to predict *the* future. Rather, it's to suggest all the possible futures—so that society can make informed decisions about where we want to go."[56]

Examples

The television show Black Mirror is a good example of science fiction that explores the darker effects that new technologies could have.[57]

Each episode features a different technology in a single episode story and explores ideas for how things might go wrong when that technology becomes widespread. Watching shows like this one (available on Netflix) is a good way to think about the ethics of new technologies that your library may be exploring.

Comic books and graphic novel can be also be a good source of exploring these ideas.[58] Many libraries have collections of comics and graphic novels—use them for your own reading as well, when keeping up with technologies.

A good example is a graphic novel by Brian K. Vaughan, Marcos Martin, and Muntsa Vicente called *Private Eye*.[59] It's a story set in Los Angeles in 2076 where the Internet has long been dismantled and abandoned. In the fictional past, all digital information about everyone was suddenly made freely available everywhere, including the most private of secrets. So, in this future, people are very aware of the value of privacy and everyone has a secret identity. It explores many sides of the importance of privacy, and won the 2015 Eisner Award for best digital/web comic.

Some have criticized science fiction of recent years for its tendency to focus mainly on dystopian scenarios.[60] There have been calls for writers to create more positive visions in their works. In 2011, Neal Stephenson launched the Hieroglyph project, meant to rally writers to create more optimistic science fiction that could inspire a new generation. This resulted in the anthology, *Hieroglyph: Stories & Visions for a Better Future,* with stories by Bruce Sterling, Cory Doctorow, Elizabeth Bear, and others.[61] Learn more about Project Hieroglyph on their website, http://hieroglyph.asu.edu/. Stories like these can help balance the dystopian views found in most science fiction.

For more about why science fiction is so useful in your exploration of the ethical and philosophical concerns related to near-future technologies, read this article by Richard MacManus: "3 Reasons Why You Should Read Science Fiction."[62]

It's a good idea to keep notes on ideas that come to mind from your experiences with popular culture and science fiction. I like to keep notes in Evernote (http://evernote.com), since it's a note-taking app that I always have with me on my phone and computer. With Evernote, you can quickly create notes in different formats—text, audio, or camera notes. We'll look at this and other note-taking apps in a future chapter.

Dealing with Information Overload

Before we move on to more sources and strategies, let's pause and talk about information overload. You're probably already feeling it if you'd read this far.

How do you keep from becoming overwhelmed? You need a system. Here are some ideas.

1. ## Use "read later" apps, together with a smart e-mail app.

    When you are processing your e-mail, skim your favorite newsletters and save those articles you want to read in a "read later" app like Pocket[63]

    or Instapaper.[64] You can quickly process e-mail and not worry about reading anything while you're processing. Don't think, "I have to read all of this and I have no time!" Save it all for later. Process quickly.

    For multimedia content, such as videos or podcasts, you can use a read-later app like Pocket to save links to them. Alternatively, you can use the book-marking system with YouTube or Vimeo to save playlists of videos to watch later. Podcast listening apps like Pocket Casts have features for marking certain episodes as favorites and also for creating lists of podcasts on various topics. Use a variety of tools that are appropriate for the type of media.

    For processing e-mail, use a client that makes it easy to quickly delete and archive messages. Some good options currently are Newton, Spark, or Inbox by Gmail.[65] With these apps, you can process much more quickly, especially on mobile devices, with swipe gestures for archiving, deleting, or scheduling an e-mail to come back to the top of your inbox on a certain date or time.

2. ## Set times for reading, viewing, or listening to what you've saved.

    Set aside certain times for reading what you've saved in Pocket or a similar app—for me it's during lunch and when I need a break from my regular work. Listen to your saved podcasts while exercising or commuting. Use the tags in Pocket and similar services to mark the best articles to make them easy to find later. For example, if you're following a particular technology, make a tag for it and mark those articles with that tag.

    Consider setting a certain day of the week, at a certain time, as your time for reading, reviewing, and listening. You can put these times in your calendar as repeating events, just as you would do for a regular meeting. In the past, I've had success with allowing myself to only listen to my favorite technology podcasts when I'm out for a walk or run in the morning. Being a geek who tends to stay glued to my screens instead of exercising, that motivates me!

If you have regular times when you are sitting in waiting rooms, waiting to pick someone up in your car, or on a long subway or bus ride, use those times for reading or listening on your smartphone. These small bits of time add up. This type of reading is not the type of work that requires extreme concentration (that will come later when you are evaluating information), you're just skimming and scanning, and getting the big picture, so it doesn't matter so much if you are interrupted.

3. Go back through what you've saved in order to curate information for others.

Be a curator of information for others—your coworkers, followers, colleagues, or team. Organizing information for others is a good way to keep yourself up to date on these topics.

If you use social media like Twitter or something similar, share articles your followers would like. For example, I currently tweet about libraries, mobile technologies, apps, e-books, the digital divide, Internet access, technology trends, and related topics.[66] My followers know to expect stories on those topics.

On a regular basis, go back through your own tweets and collect the best links. I do this in order to send out a newsletter of curated links to stories called "Mobile Apps News."[67] Once a month I look back through my tweets and collect the best stories to mention in my newsletter. I often use that time to try out new apps and read completely some of the articles that I had previously only skimmed. I don't need to worry about reading everything when I first find it, because I know I'll go back through my tweets later and read articles more in depth.

4. Use automation apps like IFTTT or Zapier.[68]

These apps make it easy to trigger certain actions in an app when something happens in a different app. For example, using IFTTT (If This, Then That), you can set up a "recipe" to save any tweet you favorite to Pocket.[69] Or you can save all of your Gmail attachments to Dropbox.[70] See the IFTTT recipes page to browse through many more interesting ways to connect apps to each other, https://ifttt.com/recipes. Zapier works in a similar way and you can browse their "zaps" here, https://zapier.com/app/explore. To learn more about IFTTT, see "IFTTT Hits The Mainstream: It's Not Just For Geeks Anymore."[71]

Both IFTTT and Zapier connect apps like Gmail, Google Drive, Twitter, Facebook, Pocket, Evernote, Wunderlist, Instagram, YouTube, Vimeo, Wordpress, and many more. There are likely to be more services like these in the future. You can experiment with setting up a few automated actions until you find the ones that have the most value for you.

5. Automate with alerts.

Another way to automate the flow of information coming to you is with alerts. Google and many article databases have alerts that you can set up to be e-mailed or otherwise notified of results that match your search.

For example, in Google Alerts (https://www.google.com/alerts), you can enter your search terms, and select how often the results should come to you (such as daily or once a week). You can choose to get results from everything, or just blogs, video, books, discussions, or other sources. Set up searches on the topics you're following and remember to cancel them when they are no longer of interest.

There are also other monitoring tools and apps. Mention (http://mention.com) is a good example. It connects to all of your social media, making it easy to respond or favorite various sources that come up in your results. It can search all of the same sources that Google does, but has better integration with your social media accounts.

Another way to automate information coming to you is with an iOS app called Hooks, https://www.gethooksapp.com. It can send you push notifications for topics you sign up for. It's designed mainly for popular culture, such as new movie alerts, but also offers alerts on many news sources and for any RSS feed.

Alert tools are always evolving. Look for the best of these and set up a few alerts that work for you.

6. Prune your sources regularly.

Stop getting information that isn't useful. It's easy to start getting too many e-mail newsletters and too much of everything. Set up a regular time, perhaps once a month, for unsubscribing and getting rid of sources in all of your various feeds. By then, you'll have a sense of which ones provide the most value.

Often, it's helpful to find one or two experts on the topics you follow and use them to keep up. Follow their social media feeds, subscribe to their newsletters—let them do the curation for you. It's easier to do this after you've been following many sources for a while—because you start to find the best experts and publications for your topics.

7. Adjust your system over time.

Once every few months, think about how your system is working for you and make adjustments. Don't wait for the perfect system or spend a lot of time tweaking the perfect system. There is none. Just pick something and try it. Later make changes and improvements to your system.

8. Use apps that synchronize data between your computers and mobile devices.

Many of the best apps, such as Pocket or Evernote, run on multiple platforms, mobile and desktop. They automatically synchronize your information so that you can start a task on your laptop, continue it on your mobile phone, later continue it on your tablet, and so on.

This makes it easy to process some information in spare moments (when you're waiting in line, or on a bus or subway). When you can process information in spare moments, when you might have been a bit bored anyway, that makes it easier to keep up. For a list of recommended apps that synchronize your data, see my blog post, "50 Best Apps for Those Who Use both Android and iOS."[72]

9. Make sure your computers and mobile devices have automated backups.

In order not to worry about losing important information, use a service like CrashPlan to back up your desktop and laptop computers to the cloud.[73] There are many services like this that run silently in the background, always backing up your data. CrashPlan makes it easy to recover data that you accidentally deleted, and easily get all of your data back if your laptop is lost, stolen, or your hard drive fails.

For mobile devices, use apps that back up your Android or iOS smartphones and tablets.[74] There are a variety of options in addition to Apple's iCloud service. Look for current articles that review the best apps for these purposes. Search for "best automated backup for iOS," or "best automated backup for Android."

If you'd like more help with learning how to use the best, most secure ways to back up and synchronize your data, take my online course, "Organize Your Life with Mobile Apps," http://nicolehennig.com/courses/organize-life-mobile-apps/. When you have backup systems in place and know how to use them, you can feel less stressed about a lost smartphone, a laptop that needs repair, or other mishap.

10. Don't worry about long-term archiving of your research on emerging technologies.

This type of information is constantly changing. You need to always be reading new material—much of it will be out of date or not so useful in a few years. So if the systems you use today for storing and organizing your information aren't around in 3–5 years, most likely it won't matter because you'll have new tools and apps and new information to track.

11. Take time off.

Earlier I mentioned some skills that are good to have for this kind of work.

(1) The ability to look at the big picture without getting bogged down in details

(2) The ability to not get overwhelmed when faced with a deluge of information

You'll never be able to read or capture everything of interest, and there is no need to. Any important topics or stories will be repeated multiple times in the media. So feel free to skip days, go on vacation, and take time off to relax away from the firehose of information. It will still be there when you return.

Once in a while you may want to delete a whole batch of e-mail newsletters, so you can feel caught up. Go ahead! Start fresh on a new day and don't worry.

12. Get a feel for the big picture

One of the advantages of processing a lot of information about new technologies is that over time you start to see trends. You get a feel for which technologies are being discussed most frequently, you read stories of how they are being used, and you start to notice which ones have fallen off the map. This kind of work is all about getting the big picture, not about going into depth in your understanding of every new technology.

Endnotes

1. Abby Marks Beale, "Skimming and Scanning: Two Important Strategies for Speeding Up Your Reading," February 4, 2013, http://www.howtolearn .com/2013/02/skimming-and-scanning-two-important-strategies-for-speeding-up -your-reading/.

2. https://cloudmagic.com/k/newton

3. https://getpocket.com

4. https://zapier.com/blog/best-bookmaking-read-it-later-app/.

5. Such as Newton, mentioned in the previous chapter, https://cloudmagic.com/ k/newton.

6. See "Saving to Pocket by Email," https://help.getpocket.com/article/ 1020-saving-to-pocket-via-email, and "How to Save Email into Evernote," https://help.evernote.com/hc/en-us/articles/209005347-How-to-save-email-into -Evernote.

7. Inbox Zero (http://inboxzero.tumblr.com/) is a technique that is focused on keeping your email inbox empty. It was invented by Merlin Mann, an independent writer based in San Francisco, http://www.merlinmann.com/.

8. Slack is a real-time messaging and archiving app for teams and workgroups, see https://slack.com/.

9. Cameron Chapman, "35 Email Newsletters to Boost Your Career in Tech," http://skillcrush.com/2016/01/20/35-email-newsletters-to-boost-your-career-in -tech/.

10. http://www.newsletterstash.com/newsletter/product_hunt_tech_digest

11. See the Feedly RSS news reader, http://feedly.com/ and the many apps on different platforms that work with it, http://feedly.com/apps.html.

12. https://medium.com

13. See the different types of Creative Commons licenses here: https:// creativecommons.org/licenses/.

14. https://mondaynote.com

15. https://backchannel.com

16. http://www.slideshare.net

17. Richard McManus, "Why following people on Twitter is broken (and what to do about it)," May 12, 2015, https://richardmacmanus.com/2015/05/12/twitter -follow/.

18. Alaina G. Levine, "How to use Twitter to enhance your conference experience," *Physics Today,* March 16, 2016, http://scitation.aip.org/content/aip/ magazine/physicstoday/news/10.1063/PT.5.9054.

19. https://hootsuite.com

20. http://tweetdeck.twitter.com

21. http://nuzzel.com

22. https://bryanalexander.org/future-trends-in-technology-and-education/

23. http://creativegood.com/gel/

24. http://www.apple.com/education/itunes-u/

25. Download iTunes. http://www.apple.com/itunes/download/.

26. iTunes U app for iOS: https://itunes.apple.com/us/app/itunes-u/ id490217893?mt=8

27. Tunesviewer Android app. http://tunesviewer.sourceforge.net

28. Coursera: https://www.coursera.org, edX: https://www.edx.org, and Udacity: https://www.udacity.com.

29. https://www.lynda.com

30. https://www.lynda.com/signup

31. Pocket Casts: http://www.shiftyjelly.com/pocketcasts/

32. Overcast: https://overcast.fm

33. See the multimedia bibliography at the end of this book for more recommended apps for podcast listening.

34. http://www.stitcher.com

35. From the show description, https://itunes.apple.com/gb/podcast/tedtalks-technology/id470624027?mt=2.

36. From the show description, https://art19.com/shows/whats-tech.

37. Johnson, Steven. *Wonderland: How Play Made the Modern World.* New York, NY: Riverhead Books, 2016.

38. See http://nicolehennig.com/podcast-literacy/ and http://www.alatechsource.org/taxonomy/term/106/.

39. https://www.captivoice.com/capti-site/

40. https://www.captivoice.com/capti-site/public/entry/download

41. https://www.captivoice.com/capti-site/public/entry/tutorials1

42. From the code4lib website: https://code4lib.org/about.

43. Rebecca O. Bagley, "How 'Unconferences' Unleash Innovative Ideas," Forbes, August 18, 2014, http://www.forbes.com/sites/rebeccabagley/2014/08/18/how-unconferences-unleash-innovative-ideas/#3b3ab8035e12.

44. http://podcamp.pbworks.com/w/page/17344268/FrontPage

45. Kaliya Hamlin, "unConferencing—how to prepare to attend an unconference," accessed December 6, 2016, http://unconference.net/unconferencing-how-to-prepare-to-attend-an-unconference/.

46. George M. Eberhart, "LITA's Top Tech Trends: Tech futurists assess the state of library-related technology," *American Libraries,* June 27, 2016, http://americanlibrariesmagazine.org/blogs/the-scoop/litas-top-tech-trends-panel-2016/.

47. http://www.psfk.com/category/millennials

48. Like this one, for example: David Bolton, "Machine Learning Is at the Very Peak of Its Hype Cycle," August 17, 206, https://arc.applause.com/2016/08/17/gartner-hype-cycle-2016-machine-learning/.

49. Gartner Hype Cycle, accessed October 11, 2016, http://www.gartner.com/technology/research/methodologies/hype-cycle.jsp.

50. http://events.technologyreview.com/emtech/16/

51. https://www.amazon.com/gp/digital/fiona/kcp-landing-page/ref=kcp_ipad_mkt_lnd

52. O'Reilly publishers is a good place to buy directly from, since they have DRM-free e-books and you can get them in multiple formats for one price (EPUB, PDF, etc.), http://shop.oreilly.com/. *Take Control Books* is another good source like that works in the same way, https://www.takecontrolbooks.com/.

53. Pic2Shop app: https://www.oclc.org/developer/gallery/pic2shop.en.html. Find more apps that connect to Worldcat here: https://www.oclc.org/developer/gallery.en.html/:F3276:/.

54. Rachel Wayne, "Why It's Important to Study Popular Culture," *LinkedIn*, July 27, 2014, https://www.linkedin.com/pulse/20140727233003-19409547-why-it-s-important-to-study-pop-culture.

55. Patrick Purdy, "From Science Fiction to Science Fact: How Design Can Influence the Future," *UX: User Experience, The Magazine of the User Experience Professionals Association*, June 2013, http://uxpamagazine.org/science-fiction-to-science-fact/.

56. Robert Sawyer, "The Purpose of Science Fiction," *Slate*, January 27, 2011, http://www.slate.com/articles/technology/future_tense/2011/01/the_purpose_of_science_fiction.html.

57. See http://www.channel4.com/programmes/black-mirror/ and http://www.imdb.com/title/tt2085059/.

58. For more thoughts on this, see "Comic Books—Connecting Us to Cultural Change," from a blog for a course at University of British Columbia called ETEC540: Text, Technologies—Community. October 28, 2012, http://blogs.ubc.ca/etec540sept12/2012/10/28/comic-books-connecting-us-to-cultural-change/.

59. Digital version available here: http://panelsyndicate.com/comics/tpeye, and print version here: https://www.amazon.com/Private-Eye-Brian-K-Vaughan/dp/1632155729. Read a review of this graphic novel here: http://noflyingnotights.com/blog/2016/06/27/private-eye/.

60. Annalee Newitz, "Dear Science Fiction Writers: Stop Being So Pessimistic!" *Smithsonian Magazine*, http://www.smithsonianmag.com/science-nature/dear-science-fiction-writers-stop-being-so-pessimistic-127226686/?no-ist.

61. Ed Finn & Kathryn Cramer, *Hieroglyph: Stories & Visions for a Better Future*, New York: William Morrow, 2014, http://hieroglyph.asu.edu/book/hieroglyph/.

62. Richard McManus, "3 Reasons Why You Should Read Science Fiction," Richardmacmanus.com, September 1, 2016, https://richardmacmanus.com/2016/09/01/read-science-fiction/.

63. https://getpocket.com

64. https://www.instapaper.com/

65. Newton, https://cloudmagic.com/k/newton, Spark, https://sparkmailapp.com/, Inbox by Gmail, https://support.google.com/inbox/answer/6067582?hl=en&ref_topic=6067565.

66. https://twitter.com/nic221

67. Subscribe to Mobile Apps News: http://nicolehennig.com/mobile-apps-news/.

68. https://ifttt.com and https://zapier.com.

69. Add the link of any tweet you favorite to Pocket queue. https://ifttt.com/recipes/124855-add-the-link-of-any-tweet-you-favorite-to-pocket-queue.

70. Save your Gmail attachments to Dropbox, https://ifttt.com/recipes/98759-save-all-your-gmail-attachments-to-dropbox.

71. Jared Newman, "IFTTT Hits the Mainstream: It's Not Just for Geeks Anymore," Fast Company, August 10, 2016, https://www.fastcompany.com/3062641/ifttt-hits-the-mainstream-its-not-just-for-geeks-anymore.

72. Nicole Hennig, "50 Best Apps for Those Who Use Both Android and iOS," http://nicolehennig.com/50-best-apps-use-android-ios/.

73. https://www.crashplan.com

74. See John Corpuz, "10 Best Android Backup Apps," Tom's Guide, October 25, 2016, http://www.tomsguide.com/us/pictures-story/633-best-android-backup-apps.html and Brad Ward, "How to back up your iPhone and iPad," Techradar, November 7, 2016, http://www.techradar.com/how-to/software/how-to-backup-iphone-ipad-1299014.

CHAPTER 3

Gathering Information: More Strategies

Look Outside Your Field or Discipline

One of the best ways to keep up with new technologies is to make it a point to follow information from fields outside of library and information science. Look beyond your usual sources and contacts to find and attend conferences, workshops, and meet-ups from other fields. Read books and articles outside your field as well.

Combining information from different fields often leads to creative ideas that result in new and innovative library services. So if you usually follow sources from the world of library and information science, try reading and attending events from topics such as the following:

- Consumer trends
- Creative thinking
- Digital anthropology, cyberanthropology, technoanthropology
- Educational technology
- Entrepreneurship and innovation
- Generational differences studies
- Participatory design
- Privacy and security

- Sociology of technology
- User experience and usability

No matter which type of library you work in, follow what other types of libraries are doing. We can all learn from each other, even if the users we serve are very different. Look also outside your own country or region— keep up with innovative ideas from libraries around the world. Follow information from any of following types of libraries.

- Academic libraries
- Archives
- Corporate libraries
- Government libraries
- Museums
- Nonprofit libraries
- Public libraries
- School libraries

In the previous chapter, I recommended some specific conferences and events (both virtual and physical) that are outside the traditional world of library science. These events are often full of ideas that you can bring into the world of library services.

Categories of Technologies

As you are investigating new technologies, it can be useful to have some categories to group them in. *The Horizon Report*, discussed in the previous chapter, has a useful grouping of categories in the 2015 Library Edition.[1] These are found in the section, "Important Developments in Technology for Academic and Research Libraries," pp. 34–35. These are described as a way to organize emerging technologies into pathways of development that may be relevant to academic and research libraries.

Consumer Technologies. These are important because people use these at home or in other settings and they can be adapted for learning. Examples: 3D video, drones, electronic publishing, quantified self, robotics, tablet computing, telepresence, and wearable technology

Digital Strategies. It's important to look at both formal and informal strategies for using devices and software to enrich learning. These can go beyond conventional ideas to create something new.

Examples: Bring your own device (BYOD), flipped classroom, location intelligence, and preservation/conservation technologies

Enabling Technologies. These are technologies that expand tools to make them more capable, useful, and easier to use.

Examples: Affective computing, flexible displays, machine learning, mesh networks, natural user interfaces, -near field communication, next-generation batteries, speech-to-speech translation, virtual assistants, and wireless power

Internet Technologies. This category includes techniques and infrastructure that help make the underlying network technologies transparent and easier to use.

Examples: Cloud computing, semantic web and linked data, and syndication tools

Learning Technologies. These are technologies developed expressly for learning.

Examples: Adaptive learning technologies, digital badges, learning analytics, mobile learning, online learning, and open licensing

Social Media Technologies. These are now so widely used in every part of society that they get their own category in the Horizon Report. They evolve at a rapid pace.

Examples: Crowdsourcing, online identity, and social networks

Visualization Technologies. These are everything from infographics, to complex visual data analysis. They tap into the brain's ability to rapidly process visual information and to sense patterns.

Examples: 3D printing, augmented reality, information visualization, and holographic displays

This is not a fixed list, so you will likely find different or new categories that work for your situation, as we move into the future. But having a list of categories like these can serve as a useful way to group your findings and they can remind you to look at a wide variety of technology types.

How Far Out to Look

Sometimes when exploring new technologies it's challenging to determine which ones are going to be important soon and which ones won't be important until a few years out. There are some useful models to look at when thinking about this—models that explain the cycles that most technologies go through. Let's look at some of those models in order to think about how far into the future to look.

1. Gartner Hype Cycle

The Gartner Hype Cycle is a model developed by the IT research firm, Gartner.[2] I mentioned this earlier in the chapter on trend reports. It's used to talk about the maturity stages of specific technologies, so that decision-makers can decide at what point to try out emerging technologies.

The stages are the following:

A. *Technology trigger.* This is the stage where a technology break-through begins. It's the stage where proof-of-concept stories get media attention. Usually, no viable products exist yet.

B. *Peak of inflated expectations.* In this stage, there are success stories that get publicity, so expectations are high.

C. *Trough of disillusionment.* Some early experiments fail to deliver in this stage, and people lose hope. Providers of the technology only survive if they improve their products so that early adopters are satisfied.

D. *Slope of enlightenment.* In this stage, the benefits of the technology start to become more widely understood. Second- and third-generation products are developed. Some people begin to use these for pilot projects, while others remain cautious.

E. *Plateau of productivity.* This is when mainstream adoption takes off. The technology becomes useful to a broad market and the relevance can clearly be seen.

There is some criticism of this model, saying that it's not really a cycle, it doesn't account for technologies that drop off the map entirely, and so on.[3] But it can be useful as a way to think about the fact that new technologies usually go through stages like these—early hype, disillusionment, and coming back in a more reliable way. It's a good reminder than many technologies take several years to mature enough to be useful. You can think about each technology that you are investigating as having a place on this curve.

2. Diffusion of Innovations

"Diffusion of Innovations" is a model that aims to explain the spread of new technologies. Everett Rogers, a professor of communication studies, popularized the theory in his book *Diffusion of Innovations*—first published in 1962, and now in its fifth edition.[4]

He proposed that four main elements influence the spread of a new technology: the innovation itself, communication channels, time, and a social system. A technology must be widely adopted in order to be sustainable.

In order to describe how people adopt new technologies, he divides them into the following groups.

- Innovators, 2.5%
- Early adopters, 13.5%
- Early majority, 34%
- Late majority, 34%
- Laggards, 16%

You've likely heard of these categories, as they are widely used today. Graphs that illustrate this model show the percentages above, with most people in the early or late majority.

According to this model,

Innovators are willing to take risks and can afford to do so because of high social status and financial means. They often have the closest contact to scientific sources and innovators.

Early adopters are opinion leaders with advanced education and a fairly high social status. They are more discreet in their choices to adopt new technologies than innovators and their careful choices help them to serve as trusted communicators about new technologies.

Early majority are those who wait significantly longer than the first two groups to adopt new technologies. They usually have above average social status and they have contact with early adopters.

Late majority are those who adopt new technologies later than the average person. They approach innovations with a high degree of skepticism and often don't have the financial means to take risks. They are usually in contact with others in the early and late majority, but not with early adopters.

Laggards are those who are the last to adopt an innovation. They typically have an aversion to change. They focus on traditional ways of doing things and usually have contact mainly with family and close friends (I don't like the negative connotation of this term, but that's what it's called in this model).

When you think about where you and your peers fall in these groups, also think about the various groups of users you serve and where they might fall. If you or someone in your organization is an early adopter, you can serve as an opinion leader to help spread adoption by the next group, the early majority. And of course, you probably realize that the "late majority" and "laggards" (Rogers' term, not mine) are going to need more time and will still be learning about technologies long after you consider them fully adopted.

3. NMC Horizon Report

The New Media Consortium is a group of universities, colleges, museums, and research centers with a mission of helping educators build on innovation happening at their institutions by providing them with expert research and analysis.[5]

Each year, they publish their Horizon Report, with separate editions for higher education, K-12, museums, and libraries.[6] Each report looks at technology impacts grouped into three categories.

- Short-term (1–2 years)
- Mid-term (3–5 years)
- Long-term (5+ years)

They divide the challenges in each of these time frames into categories called solvable, difficult, or wicked. Take a look at a recent library edition to see how this works: *2015 Library Edition*, http://cdn.nmc.org/media/2015-nmc-horizon-report-library-EN.pdf.

Their framework can be a useful one for your own investigations. In addition to reading their reports, you can categorize your own research in a similar way, with short-term, mid-term, and long-term groupings. And of course, you can use their information as a jumping off point for working out the specific trends and impacts for your own organization. Be sure to look at all of the reports—trends that impact museums and K-12 education may also be of interest to those in higher education, and vice versa.

Summary

When you think about how far out to look, you can use these models as guidance. Dividing your research into short-term, mid-term, and long-term is a simple and useful way to group things. Thinking about your users by using the list of terms from diffusion of innovations (early adopters, late majority, etc.) is also quite useful. And realizing that new technologies often go through stages as described in Gartner's Hype Cycle is also useful. Sometimes a technology that seems like it's fading away is in the "trough of disillusionment," and will later become an important, widespread trend once it's matured and made more user-friendly.

We can never precisely predict the future, but we can keep an open mind about where trends might be going by using some of these models for guidance.

Visionaries and Implementers—Strategies for Each

At the beginning of this book, I talked about two roles with different skill sets, the visionary and the implementer. Let's review their characteristics.

The Visionary

- has the ability to look at the big picture without getting bogged down in details.
- does not easily get overwhelmed when faced with a deluge of information.
- is good at thinking creatively and combining ideas from different fields.
- has a desire to be an "early adopter" (taking it in stride if things break).
- has a strong curiosity about emerging technologies and where they might lead.
- has a sense of optimism about the possibilities of new technologies.
- is a continual learner, with a love for learning.
- is good at communicating in interesting ways that grab your emotions.

The Implementer

- is good at analyzing and understanding specific details.
- is good at evaluating and organizing information.
- is good at applying the results of user needs studies.
- prefers to use new technologies after others have tested them and they are more mature and more solid.
- is good at thinking linearly and understanding cause and effect.
- has a healthy skepticism about new technologies and possible pitfalls.

- asks interesting questions about each new technology.

- is good at project management, leading teams, and making sure details get carried out correctly.

You might find yourself clearly within one of these areas according to your talents and inclinations. Or you might find yourself in between, somewhere on a continuum between them.

If you identify with the implementer, you are probably feeling over-whelmed after reading through the first few chapters of this book. There are so many methods and so many resources. The methods in the upcoming chapters of this book may be of more interest to you since they are focused on evaluating and analyzing information.

If you identify with the visionary, you are probably excited to get started, and have already bookmarked many of the resources you found here that you didn't already know about. These first chapters were probably your favorite parts of the book, even though you're interested in all of it.

Tips for Implementers

If you are feeling mostly overwhelmed with these ideas for keeping up with new and emerging technologies, here are some tips for you.

1. Find someone else to curate information for you. This may take time, but eventually you'll notice which Twitter feeds, which e-mail newsletters, and which podcasts offer you the most value. Find and subscribe to a very small number of these.

2. Unsubscribe to everything that doesn't give good value for the time you spend with it.

3. Look for people in your own organization who enjoy keeping up with everything and get occasional updates from them, perhaps in person, over lunch.

4. Attend one or two local events that show promise for summarizing the best new technologies.

5. Attend online webinars once in a while that focus on describing emerging technologies.

6. Read the summary of an important trend report, such as one of those mentioned in the trend reports section of this book.

You get the idea: focus on what you're good at—project management and evaluation. Rely on others to do the broad sweep and curate the best information for you. Create teams that include both types of people and work together.

Tips for Visionaries

If you are excited about using these ideas for keeping up, great! You are ready to put them into practice. However, here are some tips and things to keep in mind when investigating new technologies.

1. Remember that not everyone has as much enthusiasm for keeping up as you likely do. This means that you need to consider your communication style so that you can work effectively with anyone. We'll discuss this in the section on presenting to decision-makers.

2. Find ways to curate the information you are gathering and make it available to others, such as a brief newsletter or a series of informal talks. Share what you're learning on a regular basis, so others don't have to. This is a good way to solidify your own learning as well, since you need to decide what is worth sharing.

3. Find ways to talk to your "implementer" colleagues in ways that make sense to them. Show them that you have carefully considered process and methodology for trying out new technologies in a way that won't cause problems for others. Talk about how particular technologies have promise for meeting specific user needs. I'll discuss methodologies for that later in this book.

4. Make sure to discuss with your colleagues how each new technology may have positive or negative impacts on people. Be ready with both critiques and success stories, so that people can consider the whole picture. News media often favor dystopian stories, since fearful headlines draw large audiences, which sells advertising. Often people have heard many stories about the possible downsides of technologies without hearing much about the benefits.

5. Give historical context when communicating about new technologies. Every new technology had its detractors and fearful stories about outcomes when it was new (printed books, radio, and television). Be ready with a few examples of these to remind people that it's common to fear technological change.[7]

6. Remember that you may end up overwhelmed at times too, and take time out to cut down on the number of sources you are following. Occasionally, take time off from following technology news, even if you love immersing yourself in it. The important news will still be there when you return, and your mind will be fresh to consider it in new ways.

Endnotes

1. *NMC Horizon Report, 2015 Library Edition*, http://cdn.nmc.org/media/2015-nmc-horizon-report-library-EN.pdf.

2. Gartner Hype Cycle, http://www.gartner.com/technology/research/methodologies/hype-cycle.jsp.

3. Technology Hype Curve, http://demandingchange.blogspot.com/2005/09/technology-hype-curve.html.

4. Everett Rogers, *Diffusion of Innovations*, New York: Free Press, 5th edition, 2005.

5. NMC Horizon Project History, http://www.nmc.org/nmc-horizon/nmc-horizon-project-history/.

6. Download the various editions of the NMC Horizon report, http://www.nmc.org/publication-type/horizon-report/.

7. Len Wilson, "11 Examples of Fear and Suspicion of New Technologies," accessed December 6, 2016, http://lenwilson.us/11-examples-of-fear-and-suspicion-of-new-technology/.

CHAPTER 4

Gathering Information: User Needs

At the beginning of this book, I recommended keeping up with new technologies and user needs at the same time, or in an alternating fashion. By that, I meant that we shouldn't wait to study new technologies until we understand what our users need.

Of course, it's often more of a problem that someone wants to try out every new technology trend without a good idea of what will actually help users. Every section of this book so far has been focused on learning about technologies. Now, we'll turn to understanding our users.

UX: User Experience Research

The term UX (user experience) has many definitions. Here is how the UXPA (User Experience Professionals Association) defines it.

> "Every aspect of the user's interaction with a product, service, or company that make up the user's perceptions of the whole. User experience design as a discipline is concerned with all the elements that together make up that interface, including layout, visual design, text, brand, sound, and interaction. UE works to coordinate these elements to allow for the best possible interaction by users."[1]

UX is broader than just usability studies (which are focused on how well an existing product or service works for people). It's research that's open-ended and qualitative, that looks at the big picture of how people use technologies and their surrounding services.

If you are lucky, your organization has a user experience department or team, or perhaps a person assigned to that role. If you don't, you can still infuse your work with an understanding of user needs. One of the ways you can do that is to read user needs studies of people that are similar to your own users. For example, if you are in an academic library, read studies such as Nancy Fried Foster's *Studying Students: A Second Look* (Chicago: ACRL, 2013).[2] Often the results of those studies will be helpful to you because users at similar types of libraries have similar needs.

You can also conduct your own user studies from time to time. There are several techniques for this. These are not the usual library surveys that you might be used to conducting at regular intervals. Instead they are techniques that help you understand by observation rather than by asking people what they think. The results of these types of studies are complementary to your large-scale survey results and usually help to provide context in ways that surveys don't. These qualitative results can help answer the "why" questions you might have about your quantitative survey results.

Types of User Research

In addition to traditional user surveys, there are several other methods of learning about your users. While surveys require a large sample size, these methods can be done with small- to medium-sized samples and still be valid. Some of these rely on self-reporting, while others are observational. Some of these methods are quick, low-cost, and can give you valuable data right away.

Diary Studies

Participants are asked to keep a diary (structured or unstructured) over time about specific experiences. These are good for when you have a limited set of questions you want to ask, when the questions are easy to answer, and the experience is not so frequent that it will interrupt the tasks of participants when keeping a diary about it.

Interviews

These are guided conversations and can be structured or unstructured. They can be done alone, or along with one of the other types of research, such as after a diary study or card-sort. Interviewing multiple users can give you a holistic view and help you decide what other questions need to be researched.

Card Sorting

This is a test using physical or virtual cards where users are asked to sort words or concepts into groups that are meaningful to them. It's often used to guide the design of a virtual product, such as a website. When you aggregate the concepts offered by several users, you can organize your interface in ways that make sense to them.[3]

Focus Groups

With focus groups, 6–10 people are brought together for an hour or two to provide their subjective responses to questions or demonstrated products and services. The group discussion can spark more ideas than individual interviews. These are best for idea generation rather than formal evaluation. You can also discover challenges, frustrations, likes, and dislikes.

I usually don't recommend this technique, since it's more about the opinions of users rather than observations (which are more valuable). These sessions can often turn into gripe-sessions where users complain about things that you don't have the ability to change (such as the user interface of third-party databases). I would recommend doing any of the other methods in this list before conducting a focus group.

Field Studies

During a field study, a researcher visits people in their own environment and observes them in their daily tasks. These can last anywhere from a few hours to several days. These studies help you capture information that impacts your product or service in the real world, such as interruptions, distractions, and competing tasks. These studies are usually most useful when you're designing a new product or service.

Evaluation Methods

These are a group of different methods for evaluating designs of new or existing products and services. They include storyboards, paper prototypes, heuristic evaluation,[4] usability testing, heat maps,[5] and other methods. Some of these evaluations are done early in the cycle of creating a new service in order to shape the design direction. Others are done toward the end in order to make adjustments and improvements to interfaces before going live.

These brief descriptions are only a starting point, meant to give you a taste of the variety of types of research that can be done to understand users. To learn more, I recommend the following book, which served as my handbook for many years and is now in its second edition: *Understanding Your Users: A Practical Guide to User Research Methods* by Kathy Baxter, Catherine Courage, and Kelly Caine.[6] If you have access to Safari Books Online,[7] this book is available there.

Using this book, you can learn which type of study will work best for what you want to learn and follow step-by-step instructions for conducting each type of study. It's also very helpful for learning to interpret your results.

Examples

For examples of these types of studies, take a look at the following documentation of some user experience projects we did while I worked at the MIT Libraries.

Digital Scholarship Study (Diary Studies and Interviews)

In the spring of 2011, our user experience group, with help from several librarian liaisons, conducted a study of the needs of the MIT community. This study focused on how new technologies and formats were having an impact on how MIT scholars find, use, and share information for their study, research, and publishing.

Student volunteers recorded their own research behavior over the course of a one-week period using their own digital camera and taking notes in any format they wished. Our staff then conducted in-depth interviews of each participant.

Read the executive summary to learn more, http://hennigweb.com/keeping-up/dig-scholarship-summary.pdf. You may also want to take a look at presentation slides about this study from a talk I gave for the Society of Scholarly Publishers, http://www.slideshare.net/nic221/academic-ereading-themes-from-user-experience-studies.

Patron for a Day (Field Study)

This test was an opportunity for staff to learn what it is like to be a user by performing a series of tasks patrons regularly perform in our physical spaces. Some tasks required interaction with technology, such as scanners and computers, while others just required interaction with the physical space and collections. Some tasks were easy—"find the restroom"; others were harder—"scan pages from book X and send to your e-mail."

Staff members visited libraries on campus other than the one they worked in to complete their test. They were asked to take notes about their experience, and after completion, were asked to rate each task and enter their comments into a web form. We had 20 volunteers complete one of three different tests at one of four campus libraries. See our internal report for details and results, http://hennigweb.com/keeping-up/patron-for-a-day.pdf. You can see a few photos I took when I completed the test myself here, https://www.flickr.com/photos/nic221/sets/72157625306370788.[8]

Learning More about UX in Libraries

To learn more about the field of user experience and how to apply it in libraries, I recommend the following resources.

Andy Priestner and Matt Borg, editors. *User Experience in Libraries: Applying Ethnography and Human-Centred Design.* New York: Routledge, 2016. See also their website, http://uxlib.org, which offers news of related conferences and events.

Weave: Journal of Library User Experience, http://weaveux.org/. Weave is an open-access, peer-reviewed journal for library user experience professionals published by Michigan Publishing. Many useful articles are here, such as this one: "DIY Usability: Low-Barrier Solutions for the Busy Librarian," Emily Mitchell and Brandon West, volume 1, issue 5, 2016.[9]

LibUX, http://libux.co/. LibUX is the website of Michael Schofield and Amanda L. Goodman. They provide design and development consultancy for user experience departments and library web teams. Their site offers articles and podcast episodes about UX in libraries. They also offer a Slack channel, found at https://libraryux.slack.com. This is a useful place to ask questions and get advice about your user needs studies.

Designing Better Libraries, http://dbl.lishost.org/blog/. An excellent blog by Steven Bell[10] about user experience, design thinking, and creativity for libraries.

The Importance of Understanding Your Users

I highly recommend implementing users needs research in your organization. These methods that focus on observation instead of opinion can give you such valuable information that you often can't learn in other ways (such as surveys). If you understand the needs of your users, you can use technologies most effectively to help them meet their goals.

Endnotes

1. User Experience Professionals Association, "Definitions of User Experience and Usability," accessed December 6, 2016, https://uxpa.org/resources/definitions-user-experience-and-usability.

2. For example, see Nancy Fried Foster, *Studying Students: A Second Look,* Chicago: ACRL, 2013, and Nancy Fried Foster and Susan Gibbons, editors, *Studying Students: The Undergraduate Research Project at the University of Rochester,* Chicago: ACRL, 2007. Download a free copy from: http://www.ala.org/acrl/sites/ala.org.acrl/files/content/publications/booksanddigitalresources/digital/Foster-Gibbons_cmpd.pdf.

3. This can be done in person with index cards, or online with tools like *Optimal Sort,* from a company called Optimal Workshop, https://www.optimalworkshop.com/optimalsort.

4. Heuristic evaluation involves using an established checklist of recommended characteristics (heuristics), in order to see if your website, app, or service complies with each item on the list.

5. A heat map is a tool that shows which links on a web page have the most clicks during a particular time frame. This is done visually using a range of colors that make it easy to see the most-clicked areas of a page. For an example, CrazyEgg is a tool for this, https://www.crazyegg.com/.

6. Kathy Baxter, Catherine Courage, and Kelly Caine, *Understanding Your Users: A Practical Guide to User Research Methods,* Waltham, MA: Morgan Kaufmann, 2nd edition, 2015.

7. https://www.safaribooksonline.com

8. Feel free to use my photos, all are licensed with Creative Commons sharing, https://creativecommons.org/licenses/by-nc-sa/2.0/.

9. Emily Mitchell and Brandon West, "DIY Usability: Low-Barrier Solutions for the Busy Librarian," *Weave: Journal of Library User Experience,* volume 1, issue 5, 2016, http://dx.doi.org/10.3998/weave.12535642.0001.504.

10. http://stevenbell.info/

CHAPTER 5

Ethics, Inclusion, and the Digital Divide

Following Ethical Debates

With each new technology there are always moral and ethical choices related to how it will be used. There are often debates about specific technologies and how they affect society and social norms.

It's good to keep informed about specific issues that are coming up with each new technology so that you can thoughtfully consider the choices that you make about implementation and experimentation. Make it your goal to follow the ethical controversies around specific technologies, so that you can make decisions in line with your own values and the values of your organization and your profession.

As a starting point, refer to the Code of Ethics of the American Library Association, which can be found online at: http://www.ala.org/advocacy/proethics/codeofethics/codeethics. These ethics include principles such as the following:

- Aiming for the highest level of service to all

- Upholding the principles of intellectual freedom

- Protecting each user's right to privacy

- Enhancing our knowledge and skills, and encouraging professional development of coworkers.

Almost certainly your own organization has a code of ethics or similar statements. It's worth finding those and referring to them.

Tips for Following Ethical Debates Related to New Technologies

1. Look for specific articles that discuss some of the ethical red flags in near future technologies. An example: "The Many Ethical Implications of Emerging Technologies."[1]

2. Follow reports from relevant centers at universities, such as the John J. Reilly Center at the University of Notre Dame.[2] They publish a helpful list of "Emerging Ethical Dilemmas" each year. For example, here's the 2016 list: http://reillytop10.com/.[3] For an example of a specific technology, see "Wearable Technology," with their excellent resource guide to learning about the ethical issues surrounding it, http://reilly.nd.edu/outreach/emerging-ethical-dilemmas-and-policy-issues-in-science-and-technology-2015/wearable-technology/. Another useful guide summarizes the issues around 3D printing, http://reilly.nd.edu/outreach/emerging-ethical-dilemmas-and-policy-issues-in-science-and-technology/3-d-printing/.

3. Follow nonprofit groups that advocate for and report on ethical issues. A good example is EPIC, https://epic.org/. They are a public interest research center that focuses on privacy and civil liberties. You can subscribe to their e-mail alerts to keep up with the latest news related to privacy, https://epic.org/alert/. They cover issues such as big data, cloud computing, consumer privacy, cybersecurity, government surveillance, location privacy, search engine privacy, and student privacy.[4]

   Another nonprofit worth following is EFF (Electronic Frontier Foundation), https://www.eff.org. Their mission is to defend civil liberties in the digital world. They champion user privacy, free expression, and innovation. Learn more and sign up for their e-mail list here, https://www.eff.org/. The issues they cover are listed here, https://www.eff.org/issues, and include free speech, fair use, innovation, privacy, international issues, and transparency. They also provide practical information, such as their guide, "Surveillance Self-Defense: Tips, Tools and How-tos for Safer Online Communications," https://ssd.eff.org/.

4. Follow librarians and other professionals who often write about ethical issues related to technology. For example, librarian Barbara Fister's articles and book reviews[5] for *Inside Higher Ed*, often focus on these types of issues, see: https://www.insidehighered.com/users/barbara-fister.

5. Listen to podcasts that focus on the ethics of new technologies. A great example is *Note to Self*, from WNYC, http://www.wnyc.org/shows/notetoself/. Here is their show description: "Is your phone watching you? Can wexting (work texting) make you smarter? Are your kids real? These and other essential quandaries for anyone trying to preserve their humanity in the digital age. Join host Manoush Zomorodi for your weekly reminder to question everything."[6]

Several of the other podcasts mentioned in the multimedia resources section of this book cover the ethics of new technologies.

Summary

It's good to stay current with the various sides of these debates. The issues will certainly come up when you get to the stage of recommending new technologies that you might want to experiment with. No matter where you fall on the spectrum of opinions related to each technology, it's good to be informed, so you can encourage thoughtful discussion. Some of us tend to be "techno-optimists," who want to try every new technology and others "techno-skeptics," finding reasons to halt every new experiment, or simply not support even small tests of new technologies. I believe that we can find a place somewhere between those extremes, with a balanced approach, in order to move forward with innovations that are in line with our professional values.

Being Inclusive: Diversity, Accessibility, and the Digital Divide

As you gather information on new technologies, it's always important to keep diversity, accessibility, and the digital divide in mind. These are areas that are easy to overlook, especially in the world of new technologies.

It's good to be familiar with guidelines, laws, and recommendations in these areas, both nationally and in your own institution. Following are some examples.

Diversity

A good place to start is to become familiar with the diversity standards from your library associations, like these.

1. *Diversity Standards: Cultural Competency for Academic Libraries (2012)*. Association of College and Research Libraries, http://www.ala.org/acrl/standards/diversity.

For example, look at standard 4: "Librarians and library staff shall develop collections and provide programs and services that are inclusive of the needs of all persons in the community the library serves."

2. *Strategic Planning for Diversity.* American Library Association's Office for Diversity, http://www.ala.org/advocacy/diversity/workplace/diversityplanning.
This site encourages the creation of a diversity plan for your library. While you are creating your diversity plan, think about how your use of new technologies will fit into this plan. If you already have one, refer to it and use it when planning new technologies.

After you review these standards, take a look at some other sources that will spark your thinking about diversity as it relates to new technologies.

3. *Code{4}Lib Journal*, issue 28, April 15, 2015, *Special Issue on Diversity in Library Technology*, http://journal.code4lib.org/issues/issues/issue28. In this special issue the focus is on diversity. Every article in this issue is worth reading and considering. For example, "User Experience is a Social Justice Issue," by Sumana Harihareswara, looks at several examples of how bad design makes a huge difference in who can use particular technologies. From the article:

> We need to exercise a disciplined empathy. It's an empathy that includes qualitative thinking, like interviews and watching people use stuff to see where the snags are... The tech industry is not very good at empathy. I'm speaking from my own experience here–I know library tech is its own field–but in my experience, we just drop the ball on empathy and hospitality a lot. . . . The tech industry values masculinity over femininity, meaning traits like hospitality are devalued.[7]

Harihareswara goes on to recommend several user experience and usability testing resources, similar to those recommended in this book.

4. Another excellent article in that issue focuses on cultural biases built in to library classification systems and Google search algorithms. It proposes ways of applying feminist principles in the design of information services for scholars. See "Feminism and the Future of Library Discovery," by Bess Sadler and Chris Bourg in that same issue of *Code{4}Lib Journal*.[8]

5. *Model View Culture: A Magazine about Technology, Culture, and Diversity*, https://modelviewculture.com/, is another good source to follow. Here are a few sample articles, to give you an idea of what they cover. In February of 2017, Model View Culture announced that they will no longer be publishing new content. They will continue to make past issues available online, and those issues are worth reading.

- Anjuan Simmons, "Making Tech Spaces Safe for Diverse Faces," October 30, 2014, https://modelviewculture.com/pieces/making-tech-spaces-safe-for-diverse-faces.
- Lacey Williams Henschel, "Organizing More Accessible Tech Events," May 20th, 2015, https://modelviewculture.com/pieces/organizing-more-accessible-tech-events.
- Lauren Voswinkel, "Let's Talk About Pay," April 28th, 2015, https://modelviewculture.com/news/lets-talk-about-pay.

6. "Why are 'innovative' tech companies still struggling with diversity?," by Suzanne McGee in *The Guardian* (April 10, 2016), https://www.theguardian.com/technology/us-money-blog/2016/apr/10/tech-diversity-companies-recruiting-hiring. This article nicely summarizes the problems related to hiring a diverse workforce in the technology industry. Discussing the lack of diversity on the staff of Twitter, we read this:

> As of last summer, only 49 of Twitter's 2,910 employees were black, or 1.7%; 3% were black or Latino. That's a big issue for a company that is heavily issued by the black population of the US, and drew fire from the Rev Jesse Jackson, among others.

> ... the only senior black engineer at Twitter, Leslie Miley, lost his job as part of a large round of layoffs. Miley's public and candid comments about what it's like to be black and work at a senior level inside a Silicon Valley firm are both painful and crucial reading. He laid out, calmly and dispassionately, how diverse candidates were "dinged" for not having internships at "strong" companies or "not being fast enough to solve problems." Miley recounts that it took hours of lobbying to convince higher-ups to take a chance on hiring these individuals. "Needless to say, the majority of them performed well."

It's important to educate ourselves if we aren't already deeply familiar with these issues. Reading articles like these are a good place to start. See also, "The Lack Of Diversity In Tech Is A Cultural Issue," by Bonnie Marcus on Forbes.com[9] for more on the reasons for this problem.

Becoming and staying informed on diversity issues is important as you explore the world of new technologies for library services.

Accessibility

"Accessibility is the practice of accommodating multiple abilities, by making products and services easier to use for more people in more situations."[10]

This definition by Kel Smith from the excellent book, *Digital Outcasts: Moving Technology Forward without Leaving People Behind*,[11] is the most useful one I've found. Notice how it focuses on multiple abilities and on ease of use for more situations, situations that could apply to anyone.

It's a common misconception that making websites (and other technologies) accessible is something that serves only a small number of people. It's also common to think of compliance with accessibility guidelines as something that might make any new technology less beautiful or useful for those who don't need those particular features. It turns out that both ideas are false. In fact, designing accessible products and services improves the world for all of us, sometimes in unexpected ways.

A simple example is curb cuts—the feature where sidewalks have ramps leading into the street designed for use by people in wheelchairs. This is also useful for people pushing strollers or wheeled suitcases. Another example is web designs with easily resizable text—this is useful not just for those with low vision but for people viewing a web page on a presentation screen from the back of a crowded room.

Voice input on mobile devices was designed for people who are blind or have low vision. It allows people to speak into their device and have their voice translated to text. This is handy for all of us. If you hate typing on a small screen, it's incredibly useful to just speak to your device and then fix any words it gets wrong. I know people who do all of their text messaging this way, rather than typing everything. If you haven't tried it, it's worth turning on this feature.[12]

This happens often—making technology design more accessible has unexpected benefits for all of us. Considering accessible design as an important part of technology projects right from the start is a way to make things easier to use for everyone—something that I know information professionals feel strongly about, whether you are mandated to by law[13] or you just want to do the right thing.

One bit of good news is that with the move to mobile devices, with touch screens, voice input, and camera input, there are many benefits for people with all kinds of abilities or disabilities. This user interface design trend is known as "NUI," which stands for "natural user interface."[14] This is a move forward from "GUI," or "graphical user interface," which required a mouse or trackpad and the visual metaphor of a desktop with icons and menus. It's a step that makes devices like the iPad easy to figure out for the first time, by everyone from toddlers to the elderly.

For example, read this inspiring story about how the Apple Watch is making life easier for a young woman with Usher Syndrome: Molly Watt, "My Apple Watch after 5 days!" April 29, 2015,

http://www.mollywatt.com/blog/entry/my-apple-watch-after-5-days.
Here's part of what she has to say:

> So far for me the most useful app on the Apple Watch is Maps – on my iPhone
> I can plan my journey from one destination to another, for me it will be on foot
> with Unis my guidedog. This is where Haptics really come into its own – I can
> be directed without hearing or sight, but by a series of taps via the watch onto
> my wrist – 12 taps means turn right at the junction or 3 pairs of 2 taps means
> turn left, I'm still experimenting with this but so far very impressed – Usher
> Syndrome accessible![15]

Another benefit of this trend is that devices that most people consider
"cool," like an iPad, can be used in place of previously expensive,
clunky devices that marked a person as different because of their
disability.

> One of the key challenges for a person with a disability is to be seen by the
> public, to be portrayed in media outlets, and treated by health care profes-
> sionals, as an individual with their own abilities, not just stereotyped as a
> "disabled person."

From the home page of Disabled World, https://www.disabled-world
.com/.

For an inspiring story of how the use of an iPad has helped a teenaged
autistic boy, see the two videos on this page, http://bridgingapps.org/2016/
04/dillians-success-story-apple-features-autistic-teen-tech-changed-life
-3/, especially the second one.[16] Previously unable to speak, which gave
many people the impression that he lacked intelligence, he now uses an
iPad app that helps people speak, so he is now able to communicate
clearly in complete sentences.

His story is from Bridging Apps (http://bridgingapps.org), an excellent
website on the power of using touch-based technology with proper training to impact the lives of people with disabilities. It's a community of
parents, teachers, therapists, and doctors who share information.
Take a look at their section of success stories, http://bridgingapps.org/
success-stories/, their app search tool, https://search.bridgingapps.org/
dashboard, and their resources for seniors, http://bridgingapps.org/
seniors/. They also have a free course on mobile devices for special
needs, https://www.udemy.com/getting-started-with-mobile-devices-for
-special-needs/.

With these success stories in mind, I hope you can see how important
it is to bring an awareness of accessibility best practices into every new
technology that you are considering for use in library services.

Here are a few more resources worth referring to.

Web AIM: Web Accessibility in Mind, Center for Persons with Disabilities, Utah State University, http://webaim.org/.
This site is a good resource that promotes making web content accessible to people with disabilities. Their introduction page is a good overview for anyone who is getting familiar with this topic, http://webaim.org/intro/.

Digital Accessibility Laws Around the Globe, Law Office of Lainey Feingold, updated March 29, 2016, http://www.lflegal.com/2013/05/gaad-legal/.
This site is a useful summary of accessibility laws, sorted alphabetically by country, with links for learning more in each section. An example of some useful information linked from here is "21st Century Communications and Video Accessibility Act (2010 law addressing captioning, audio description, and mobile browsers)," http://www.fcc.gov/encyclopedia/twenty-first-century-communications-and-video-accessibility-act-0.

I recommend reading the entire book mentioned at the beginning of this section: *Digital Outcasts: Moving Technology Forward without Leaving People Behind* by Kel Smith. It will help you better understand universal design and how people with disabilities actually use technology. It also contains inspiring stories of how innovation happened because of work that people did to make a technology easier to use for those with disabilities—and how that benefits everyone.

It's good to have familiarity with accessibility information, even if you don't work directly with implementing new technologies. You can advise technology implementers on your staff to use accessibility guidelines and to stay in compliance with laws affecting your region, such as the Americans with Disabilities Act, https://www.ada.gov/.

The Digital Divide

This is a topic that I know information professionals feel strongly about. One of the best sources I've found for thinking about solutions is this book, *Without a Net: Librarians Bridging the Digital Divide,* by Jessamyn C. West.[17] The author's website about the book is an excellent resource on this topic, and includes related websites, handouts and presentations, and a useful bibliography, http://www.librarian.net/digitaldivide/.

The Pew Research Center for Internet, Science, and Tech is a great place to keep up with statistics related to the digital divide, http://www.pewinternet.org/. See their list of topics, http://www.pewinternet.org/topics/, for reports on the digital divide, http://www.pewinternet.org/topics/

digital-divide/, emerging technology impacts, http://www.pew internet.org/topics/emerging-technology-impacts/, and other topics, such as statistics on particular groups—for example, African Americans, http://www.pewinternet.org/topics/african-americans/. Statistics like these are helpful when you need to make your case for additional funding.

In 2014, The Aspen Institute Dialogue on Public Libraries made this report available, "Rising to the Challenge: Re-Envisioning Public Libraries."[18] You can download a copy of the report, along with an action guide here, http://www.libraryvision.org/libraries_are_bridging_the_digital_divide_in_cities. As ways to address the digital divide, it recommends the following:

- Aligning library services in support of community goals
- Providing access to content in all formats
- Ensuring long-term sustainability for public libraries
- Cultivating leadership in your communities

This is worth reading, no matter what kind of library you work in, because the principles are similar. Some of their points worth considering as they apply to emerging technologies are the following:

- People need lifelong access to ever-changing information in order for their skills to remain relevant.
- People find it useful to learn in small, quick doses, rather than wading through piles of data that provide too much information and too little knowledge.
- People need the ability to process information in many different formats, like text, data, audio, and video—and they also need to evaluate the quality of information from different sources.
- People need places to gather, collaborate, and contribute to developing knowledge.
- People need access to conversations among creative people in their areas of interest, so that they can innovate.

Keep these needs in mind as you design new services with emerging technologies in your library.

Summary

I hope that you've recognized yourself and your colleagues on the continuum between visionary and implementer. You can use this idea as a framework to help you divide work roles, and to effectively communicate about it.

We've discussed quite a few methods for gathering information: skimming and scanning, subscribing to information sources in various formats, dealing with information overload, gathering information from outside your field, attending conferences and local events, reading trend reports, reading book summaries and how to read effectively, learning from popular culture and science fiction, deciding how far out to look, useful categories of technologies, being inclusive, accessibility, the digital divide, and gathering information about user needs.

I've also offered different strategies depending on whether you identify more with the visionary or the implementer role.

In the next few chapters of this book, I'll discuss what to do next. We'll talk about using a process called "design thinking" for moving through stages that lead to experimentation and decision-making. We'll look at how to combine trends with what you know about your users, how to design small experiments and analyze them, how to develop criteria for evaluating your experiments, and how to decide which technologies *not* to go further with. Finally, we'll look at presenting to and persuading the decision-makers who will give you time or funding, and passing on projects to implementers.

Endnotes

1. Nayef Al-Rodhan, "The Many Ethical Implications of Emerging Technologies," Scientific American, March 13, 2015, https://www.scientificamerican.com/article/the-many-ethical-implications-of-emerging-technologies/.

2. http://reilly.nd.edu/

3. See also these previous years: 2013, http://reilly.nd.edu/outreach/emerging-ethical-dilemmas-and-policy-issues-in-science-and-technology/. 2014, http://reilly.nd.edu/outreach/emerging-ethical-dilemmas-and-policy-issues-in-science-and-technology-2014/. 2015, http://reilly.nd.edu/outreach/emerging-ethical-dilemmas-and-policy-issues-in-science-and-technology-2015/.

4. See their complete list of privacy topics, https://epic.org/privacy/.

5. Barbara Fister, Book review of *Weapons of Math Destruction: The Dark Side of Big Data,* by Cathy O'Neil, *Inside Higher Ed,* September 21, 2016, https://www.insidehighered.com/blogs/library-babel-fish/weapons-math-destruction-dark-side-big-data.

6. From the show description, http://www.wnyc.org/shows/notetoself/.

7. Sumana Harihareswara, "User Experience is a Social Justice Issue," *Code4Lib Journal*, issue 28, April 15, 2015, http://journal.code4lib.org/articles/10482.

8. Bess Sadler and Chris Bourg, "Feminism and the Future of Library Discovery," *Code4Lib Journal*, ssue 28, April 15, 2015, http://journal.code4lib.org/articles/10425.

9. Bonnie Marcus, "The Lack Of Diversity In Tech Is A Cultural Issue," Forbes, August 12, 2015, http://www.forbes.com/sites/bonniemarcus/2015/08/12/the -lack-of-diversity-in-tech-is-a-cultural-issue/#60519ea63577.

10. Kel Smith, *Digital Outcasts: Moving Technology Forward without Leaving People Behind,* (Kindle Locations 399–400). Elsevier Science. Kindle Edition, 2013.

11. Ibid.

12. Luke Filipowicz, "How to enable, use, and disable dictation on iPhone and iPad," iMore, September 22, 2016, http://www.imore.com/how-enable-use-and -disable-dictation-iphone-and-ipad. Also see "Use Voice Dictation to Save Time on Android, iPhone, and iPad," How-to Geek, accessed December 6, 2016, http:// www.howtogeek.com/177387/use-voice-dictation-to-save-time-on-android -iphone-and-ipad/.

13. The Americans with Disabilities Act, https://www.ada.gov/.

14. To learn about NUI, see this book by Daniel Wigdor, *Brave NUI World: Designing Natural User Interfaces for Touch and Gesture,* Waltham, MA: Morgan Kaufmann, 2011.

15. Molly Watt, "My Apple Watch after 5 days!" April 29, 2015, http:// www.mollywatt.com/blog/entry/my-apple-watch-after-5-days.

16. Amy Barry, "Dillian's Success Story, Apple Features Teen with Autism and How the iPad Has Changed His Life," *Bridging Apps*, April 5, 2016, http:// bridgingapps.org/2016/04/dillians-success-story-apple-features-autistic-teen -tech-changed-life-3/.

17. Jessamyn C. West, *Without a Net: Librarians Bridging the Digital Divide,* Santa Barbara, CA: Libraries Unlimited, 2011.

18. Amy K. Garmer, "Rising to the Challenge: Re-Envisioning Public Libraries," Aspen Institute Communications and Society Program, 2014, http:// www.libraryvision.org/libraries_are_bridging_the_digital_divide_in_cities.

CHAPTER 6

Evaluating Information

Introduction

Now that we've looked at many ways to gather information, let's focus on evaluating and analyzing it. The goal is to figure out which new technologies are worth experimenting with and how they might meet the needs of your users.

We'll look at ideas for taking notes, curating information, how to spot trends, and distinguish trends from fads. We'll then look at a process for coming up with ideas for services that solve user problems, called "design thinking." We'll also discuss methods such as "agile," and "the lean startup." We'll look at several methods for generating creative ideas from what you've learned about technologies.

After that, we'll focus on how to set up experiments, make time and space for hands-on play, and how to evaluate the results of your experiments. And we'll talk about incorporating what you know about your users in order to design services that improve their lives.

This is a continuing cycle where you will likely have different technology project ideas in different stages simultaneously. The good news is that your experiments can give you enough information to decide whether larger projects are worth pursuing.

We'll then move on to deciding what to "graveyard" (which of your tech experiments not to bother with), and how to decide which technologies are worth incorporating into library services.

In most libraries, you'll need to persuade and present to decision-makers who control your budgets and assign staff. You will learn how to effectively make a case for new services with those technologies that show the most promise for your users and that fit in with your library's strategic goals.

We'll conclude with how to best pass on projects to implementers, so that the visionaries can go back to the beginning of the cycle again—continuing the process of keeping up with what's new.

Letting Ideas Percolate

One of the first things to do after consuming a large amount of information about new technologies is to get away from it. Sleep on it. You need time for ideas to percolate and for your mind to come up with the kinds of creative thoughts that are more likely to arise during a walk in the woods than while sitting at your computer.

Studies say that daydreaming is a normal, beneficial cognitive function.[1] And that "mind wandering may be part of a larger class of mental phenomena that enable executive processes to occur without diminishing the potential contribution of the default network for creative thought and mental simulation."[2]

In other words, you're more likely to come up with creative ideas when you're doing something monotonous.[3] When your mind goes on autopilot, it frees up your unconscious to sift through ideas and make associations. This will help you come up with ideas for innovative uses of new technologies that you can later turn into experiments and possibly a new library service.

Find ways to capture creative thoughts that come to you while walking, exercising, showering, or daydreaming. Use any kind of note-taking tool or app that makes it convenient to capture ideas quickly. When I'm at home I like to use tools that let me speak out loud, such as my Amazon Echo.[4] I can speak items into a list that I can refer to later on my phone or computer.[5] Evernote is another good app that makes it easy to speak audio notes into your mobile devices and have them synced into your desktop version of the app.[6] You can often find some of your most creative ideas springing up at random times, so it's good to have a way to capture them.

Note-Taking

While we're on the topic of capturing ideas, let's take a look at some different ways to take notes. These days there are many more options than simply writing things down on paper (though that is still useful, of course).

Use Mobile Apps That Synchronize across Devices

Since we have mobile devices that are usually with us, it's good to take advantage of apps and services that make it easy to synchronize all of your information across your devices (smartphone, tablet, laptop, and desktop). Evernote, Microsoft One Note, Google Keep, and Simple Note are all good options that work on many devices and platforms.[7] There are sure to be other options in the future. I have found it most useful to pick just one of these apps (Evernote) and stick with it, so that I know where to find all of my notes for different projects. Any of the apps mentioned here are good options and have free versions for iOS, Android, Mac, and Windows, so they work even if you have devices of different platforms.

Evernote is a good example of this type of app. On your smartphone, you can input your notes in several ways, by typing, speaking, capturing an image with your camera, or drawing on the screen with your finger or a stylus. You can group your notes into notebooks by topic, and assign multiple tags to each note. This makes it easy to search through your notes later to find exactly what you're looking for. Your notes will synchronize across all of your devices, so you can capture notes anytime, anywhere on your phone, tablet, or computer.

Use Scanning Apps for Your Paper Notes

If you like to write by hand in a notebook, you can easily snap an image of your notes with your smartphone and save them in Evernote (or similar app). That way if you lose your paper notes or you don't have them with you, you still have a digital copy. Using a dedicated scanning app is even better, because with those you can create multipage PDFs of your notes, and even make your handwritten notes searchable (usually with the pro versions of these apps). There are several good scanning apps available such as Genius Scan,[8] JotNot Pro,[9] Scanbot,[10] and Scantastic.[11] I like the ease of use of Scanbot, but I don't think it matters which one you choose, because they are all high-quality apps (available for both iOS and Android). Most of these apps can save your scans to cloud services, such as Dropbox or Google Drive, for backing up your notes off your device.

Visual Notes: "Sketchnoting"

Writing and typing isn't the only way to take notes. Visual note-taking is another popular way to capture your thoughts and ideas. One form of this is called "sketchnoting," as defined by designer Mike Rohde, who has written some of the best books on this topic.[12] These notes combine writing and drawing to summarize ideas and explain concepts, in order to make a visual document that is easy for others to quickly scan and understand. It also helps you (as the creator of these notes) to more thoroughly digest and understand ideas.

Some people keep a personal journal of visual ideas this way. Others do sketchnoting during live conference presentations on a very large poster, making it available for people after each session—you'll see this at big conferences like South by Southwest.[13] It can also be helpful in small group meetings as a way to clarify ideas. You can use it to brainstorm ideas and to clearly explain ideas to others. To see some examples of sketchnotes, take a look at "Google I/O 2016 Keynote Sketchnote by Chiu-Ki Chan," Sketchnote Army, November 7, 2016, http://sketchnotearmy.com/blog/2016/11/7/google-io-2016-keynote-sketchnote-by-chiu-ki-chan.html.

It takes a bit of training to develop your visual style, and there are courses and books that help you learn to do this. In addition to the books mentioned above, there is an excellent online course from Creative Live that teaches this method, see "Visual Notetaking: A Beginner's Guide to Sketchnotes," by Giselle Chow: https://www.creativelive.com/courses/visual-notetaking-a-beginners-guide-to-sketchnotes-with-giselle-chow.

For more resources and examples, see "50+ Awesome Resources to Create Visual Notes, Graphic Recordings & Sketchnotes," by Laura Busche, https://creativemarket.com/blog/50-awesome-resources-to-create-visual-notes-graphic-recordings-sketchnotes. Another good book on the topic is *Unfolding the Napkin: The Hands-On Method for Solving Complex Problems with Simple Pictures* by Dan Roam, https://www.amazon.com/dp/B002YKOX8Y/.

Visual Notes: Mind Mapping

Mind mapping is a type of visual diagram that you can create in order to organize information in a way that makes it easy to see ideas at a glance. Mind maps usually begin with naming a central concept in the middle of your paper or screen, and then drawing lines out to create branches for subcategories. It's different than creating a traditional outline (which lends itself to viewing in a certain order)—instead you can show everything radiating out from the center on one page. It was popularized by British author and education consultant Tony Buzan in the mid-1970s, but the method itself goes back to the third century when philosopher Porphyry of Tyre used it to graphically visualize the concepts of Aristotle.[14]

See Buzan's books, *The Mind Map Book: How to Use Radiant Thinking to Maximize Your Brain's Untapped Potential*[15] and *The Ultimate Book of Mind Maps*,[16] for useful instructions on the technique. You can use mind-mapping informally to work through and brainstorm ideas on your own, or you can use it more formally to create maps of information for use by others to explain concepts.

There are software packages and mobile apps that can be used to create mind maps digitally. Using a tablet is a fun way to create these, because of the intuitiveness of drawing on a screen with your finger or a stylus. I like to use an iOS app called Popplet,[17] because it's so easy to use. You can easily incorporate words, lines, and images to create your mind maps. It's available for iPad and for the web.[18] For more mind mapping apps for iOS, see "Mind Mapping Apps," from AppAdvice, http://appadvice.com/appguides/show/mind-mapping-apps. If you're using Android, try SimpleMind, which gets very good reviews.[19] For more mind-mapping apps for Android, see "The top five mind mapping apps for the Android tablet."[20]

Summary

Each of these methods for capturing your ideas can be useful for reviewing your ideas, and thinking creatively. It's worth trying various methods to see which ones have value for you. Many people like the visual methods even if they feel they have no artistic skills. It's possible to learn a basic visual vocabulary of shapes that will make these methods easy to use. At the simplest level, just make sure you have a way to capture ideas when they come to you (keeping a small paper notebook at hand is fine).

Curating Information for Others

If you are an emerging technologies librarian, or want to play a similar role in your organization, it's a good idea to find ways to curate information about new technologies for your colleagues. There are several ways you could do this.

- Use Twitter as a way to tweet important stories and news.

- Use other social media to curate technology news, such as Facebook, Instagram, or Pinterest.

- Use different types of curation tools, such as Scoop.It or Paper.li.[21] New tools like this are always coming along.

- Offer an e-mail newsletter, or write a regular column in e-mail newsletters that your colleagues read.

- Create an online course that teaches others about new technologies.

- Offer webinars for librarian groups and consortiums.

- Host informal events where you can update your colleagues on what's new. Do this virtually (with Google Hangouts for example),[22] or in person, with brown bag lunches or other types of informal gatherings. This can be a fun way to share what you've learned at conferences and help you find time to go over all the new ideas you are hearing about.

Not only does this kind of curation help educate and inform others, but it's a great way to filter and expand on what you're learning in order to decide what's important enough to spread the word about. I'm sure you've experienced that you learn a great deal by teaching others about a topic. Sometimes it's just because it gives you a reason to spend more time with the topic and to learn enough to make concepts understandable to others.

Here are some examples of the ways I curate technology information. You may feel inspired to curate information in several or all of these ways as you move forward with this kind of work.

1. *Twitter.* When I see interesting news stories on topics of interest to my followers (librarians and educators), I tweet them.[23] I use Buffer[24] to schedule my tweets at intervals throughout the day, giving more people a chance to see them.

2. *E-mail newsletter.* Once a month I go back through the stories I've tweeted and pull out the best of them to include in a newsletter that I call Mobile Apps News.[25] I divide the stories into subtopics, such as New Apps, App Updates, App Lists, Just for Fun, Tips, Accessibility, Thought-Provoking, Interesting Stats, and Future. For each of the links to stories, I write a very short summary. The idea is to make it easy to scan, so people don't have to click through to read every story (except what particularly interests them), but can still learn something by reading the titles and descriptions. Subscribers have written to tell me how useful this is for them.[26] I use a popular provider called Mailchimp[27] for managing my e-mail list. There are other good options for this as well, such as Constant Contact[28] or TinyLetter[29] (a free version of Mailchimp designed for those who don't need the business features).

3. *Pinterest.* For some types of information and for some audiences, social media that focuses on images is useful. I know that many school librarians use Pinterest to share ideas and lesson plans. I curate a few boards such as "Content Creation with Mobile Apps,"[30] "Mobile Apps for Education,"[31] and "Infographics."[32] It makes sense to use this medium for the types of information where the visuals are primary, such as charts, graphs, infographics, and so on.

4. *Scoop.it!.*[33] This service makes it easy to create a "scoop" on a particular topic that others can follow, with the option to send your updates via e-mail. I've created a topic called Ebooks and Libraries, http://www.scoop.it/t/ebooks-libraries. You can select your favorite blogs, Twitter feeds, and other sources to choose stories from and then quickly select relevant stories from those to add to your topic. I follow a few topics that others have created and find it to be a good source of interesting news on those topics—especially since it comes to my e-mail, so I don't forget to look at it. You can see the topics I follow

here, http://www.scoop.it/u/nicole-hennig/followed-topics (Daring Ed Tech, Innovative Libraries, Learning with Mobile Devices, etc.).

5. *Online courses and webinars.* You can offer online courses or webinars through the American Library Association and other library professional organizations.[34] Many library schools also provide continuing education online where you can offer your courses. Regional library associations are known for providing webinars to their audiences on a regular basis.[35] And there are platforms where you can offer courses on your own, such as Udemy or Teachable.[36] I have in the past offered courses through Simmons GSLIS, American Library Association, and Udemy.[37] My most popular course, which I began offering in 2012 and have updated every year since then, is *Apps for Librarians and Educators,* http://nicolehennig.com/librarian -app-experts/. Like most of my courses, I offer two versions, one that happens over a five-week period via ALA E-Learning, and another version that people can take anytime, on-demand, via Udemy.[38] When you teach on Udemy, your course appears in their marketplace and you can link to it from your own sites and social media. Your students can start learning right away and have ongoing access to your course, which you can update as often as you like. Learn more about teaching on Udemy here, https://teach.udemy.com/?tc= referrers.instructoraff.NicoleHennig.

Webinars can be easier to put together than an entire five-week course. Most often you create a slide presentation and present it live using platforms like WebEx,[39] GoToMeeting,[40] or Adobe Connect.[41] These platforms usually offer a live chat session for attendees and sometimes feature polls where your audience can weigh in on questions that you create. Many regional library associations offer a series of webinars to their local information professionals, and they provide the software platform for your presentations. It's important to use a good-quality microphone when you present this way—it can make a huge difference in sound quality for the people attending. It's also a good idea to find ways to make your presentation as interactive as possible, with specific questions for your audience in the live chat, and poll questions if they make sense for your topic. I've presented webinars on various technology topics, such as "Advancing Accessibility with Mobile Devices," and "Organize Your Life with Mobile Apps."[42]

Online teaching is popular these days, especially since many people don't have large travel budgets for attending conferences. In addition, new platform providers for teaching your own courses online are appearing every year. One that gets good reviews is Teachable,[43] which offers the possibility of hosting your courses under your own domain name. No matter what the platform, online teaching is a great opportunity to curate information for other information professionals and by doing so, keep yourself up to date.

Summary

I hope you can find ways to be a curator for others if you are an emerging technologies librarian. It's a great way to become known as the expert, to save time for your busy colleagues, and to reinforce your own learning.

Trends versus Fads

While you've been analyzing all of this information, both about new technologies and about your users and what problems they face, you've probably started to notice certain technologies that look promising as solutions that could help your users.

But how do you tell which emerging technologies will really catch on and which will turn out to be just temporary fads? Sometimes a technology that everyone is experimenting with fades out after a short time. For every new technology that you are interested in exploring, you will likely encounter naysayers who say it's just a fad and will never work.

There is no foolproof method for this, but you can try some methods that have been useful to others. Let's start with a few tips for how to spot trends in the first place.

Spotting Trends Early

According to high-tech trends-spotters,[44] there are some fruitful places to look in order to spot technology trends early.

First, look at small communities of enthusiasts. For example, Bitcoin was being discussed by cryptography experts in their own communities as early as 2008.[45] By 2016, cryptocurrencies (the broader category that Bitcoin falls into), and the blockchain protocol that underlies Bitcoin are being discussed as an important technology development in places like Fortune[46] and the New York Times.[47] The blockchain protocol is now a technology that experts agree will enable trusted transactions in our digital world without the need for third parties, such as payment processors. To learn more, see "The Blockchain: What It Is and Why It Matters," in a story from the Brooking Institute, https://www.brookings.edu/blog/tech tank/2015/01/13/the-blockchain-what-it-is-and-why-it-matters/.

Where do you find these enthusiasts? Try following Kickstarter[48] projects, new Slack channels,[49] and Reddit discussions (especially fast-growing sub-Reddits)[50]. Follow the blogs and social media accounts of particular technology experts that you come across.

Another way to stay informed is to network with people who are well-connected in the communities you want to watch. Look outside your normal networks. Early adopters are often people who are open-minded, scientific, and have the time to try new things.[51] They tend to be extroverts with a lot of social ties. College campuses are a good place to start, as well as local Meetup groups, found on https://www.meetup.com/.[52]

You might also try looking at communities that have influence with new technologies. Follow programmers on sites like Stack Overflow[53] or Hacker News.[54] The opinions of programmers often determine whether a technology gets built or not.

How to Tell a Trend from a Fad

Once you are following some particular trends, there are a few ways to try to figure out which ones will stick. According to experts,[55] do the following:

1. Compare leading indicators (such as how much users care, how much better it is than alternatives, there is a large volume of positive discussion about it) with lagging indicators (such as brand recognition and prestige). If these are mismatched, that's a good sign. For example, look for situations where users and developers are crazy about a new technology and discussing it frequently, but the mainstream media doesn't seem to care yet, or notice it.

2. Look for signs of rapid and sustained growth of people using the technology.

Keep in mind that rapid growth can also happen with fads, such as Internet memes like the "ice bucket challenge." So that's not the only criteria. What you want to look for is evidence of a new discovery underlying the technology, making something new possible where it wasn't before. An example would be the trend of ride-sharing apps. These apps became a real trend because they are enabled by the new technology of smartphones, and by the fact that most people have them. A good place to keep up with technology discoveries is a report that I mentioned in the Trend Reports section called "10 Breakthrough Technologies," which comes out from *MIT Technology Review* each year.[56]

More Ideas on Spotting Trends

Kevin Kelly,[57] the author of *The Inevitable: Understanding the Twelve Technological Forces That Will Shape Our Future*,[58] has some ideas worth looking at when it comes to spotting trends and making sense of them.

First, he emphasizes that we should predict the present (instead of the future), because the future will be an extension of now. What's happening now will extend into the future.

Second, he has several specific suggestions for how to predict what's coming.

1. Follow the free
   Projects that people do for passion, where money isn't involved, often turn out to be successes later, with financial support either commercially or as a nonprofit. Wikipedia is an example.

2. Attention wastage
   Activities that seem like merely a waste of time at first often turn into the next big thing. Online gaming and the creation of animated GIFs are examples.[59]

3. New slang
   Go where there is a lot of slang. When new technologies emerge, new words appear. A term like "doxxing" is an example.[60]

4. Extrapolations
   Imagine what will happen if you take something and multiply it. For example, screens are getting thinner. If they keep getting thinner, they might be on paper or other flexible material.[61] TV screens are getting larger—multiply this and you see that there are screens that fill up entire walls of buildings or that are projected on the sky.[62] This way of thinking can lead to nonsense, but we can also find grains of truth with this method.

5. White spaces
   Look for empty areas between two known things, where there should be something, but there is currently nothing there. For example, take robots and knitting. What could end up in-between?—computational knitting,[63] with robots inventing new kinds of stitches.

6. Scenarios
   Create a set of plausible scenarios in order to come up with a set of boundaries. What's likely to happen in the future is somewhere within those boundaries of plausibility. For example, for driverless cars in the next 15 years, some plausible scenarios are: Maybe 50% of cars will be self-driving. Maybe only particular countries will have self-driving cars. Maybe only long-distance trucks will be self-driving. What's not plausible is that we will all teleport everywhere. When you make up scenarios and imagine their outcomes, this can help you rehearse for a future because you know that what's likely to happen is within those boundaries.

7. Generalize

   For a trend that is appearing, ask "what's the general principle here?"
   For example, you notice a trend where young people seem not to care
   as much as previous generations about driving or owning a car.
   The general principle is a move away from ownership to access.
   Access is more convenient than ownership (with Uber, Airbnb,
   coworking spaces, and other forms of the "sharing economy"[64]).

Kelly discusses several other ideas for predicting the future in addition to
these. I recommend reading his book *The Inevitable*, for more intriguing
ideas about our technological future. If you don't have time to read the
whole book, try listening to this audio podcast where he is interviewed:
"James Altucher, Episode 173 – Kevin Kelly: One Rule for Predicting
What You Never Saw Coming."[65]

So as you can see, there are some ideas that can help you spot trends and
determine which ones will be worth pursuing. The way to find out which
technologies have the most promise for your users is to set up small
experiments and evaluate them. We'll talk about how to do that in the next
chapter.

Summary

After you've been taking notes, reviewing information, and curating it for
others, you've probably got some ideas for which technologies are worth
looking into for library services. You still aren't ready to jump right to
implementation, though. First, it's a good idea to work with your
coworkers to learn more through hands-on play and by setting up small
experiments with technologies you are considering.

In the next chapter, I'll discuss ideas for hands-on play, designing experiments, and evaluating them. We'll also look at a methodology called
"design thinking," which is a useful way to match technologies with the
needs of your users. We'll look at how design thinking is different from
other methods, such as "agile" and "the lean startup," and what each
method is best for. I'll follow that with a section on ideation methods—
fun and interesting techniques for generating ideas to solve user problems
with technologies.

Endnotes

1. "Science of Daydreaming," Dartmouth Undergraduate Journal of Science,
February 3, 2011, http://dujs.dartmouth.edu/2011/02/science-of-daydreaming/
#.WBT6uOErLdR.

2. K. Christoff, A. M. Gordon, J. Smallwood, R. Smith, J. W. Schooler, "Experience sampling during fMRI reveals default network and executive system contributions to mind wandering," *PNAS* 106, 8719–8724, 2009.

3. Lucas Reilly, "Why Do Our Best Ideas Come to Us in the Shower?" Mental Floss, September 6, 2013, http://mentalfloss.com/article/52586/why-do-our-best-ideas-come-us-shower.

4. https://www.amazon.com/Amazon-Echo-Bluetooth-Speaker-with-WiFi-Alexa/dp/B00X4WHP5E/

5. "Manage Lists with Your Voice," Amazon Help & Customer Service, accessed December 6, 2016, https://www.amazon.com/gp/help/customer/display.html?nodeId=201549900.

6. Taylor Pipes, "Capture, Record Audio Into Evernote From Anywhere," Evernote Blog, January 7, 2015, https://blog.evernote.com/blog/2015/01/07/capture-record-audio-evernote-device/.

7. Evernote, https://evernote.com/, Microsoft OneNote, https://www.onenote.com/, Google Keep, https://keep.google.com, and Simplenote, https://simplenote.com/.

8. http://www.thegrizzlylabs.com/genius-scan/

9. http://www.jotnot.com/scanner.html

10. https://scanbot.io/en/index.html

11. http://scantastic.smoca.ch/

12. Mike Rohde, *The Sketchnote Workbook,* Peachpit Press, 2014, and *The Sketchnote Handbook*, Peachpit Press, 2012, http://rohdesign.com/.

13. https://www.sxsw.com/

14. "The Roots of Visual Mind-Mapping," The Mind-Mapping.org Blog, accessed December 6, 2016, http://www.mind-mapping.org/blog/mapping-history/roots-of-visual-mapping/.

15. Tony Buzan and Barry Buzan, *The Mind Map Book: How to Use Radiant Thinking to Maximize Your Brain's Untapped Potential*, New York: Dutton, 1994.

16. Tony Buzan, *The Ultimate Book of Mind Maps: Unlock Your Creativity, Boost Your Memory, Change Your Life,* London: HarperThorsons, 2005.

17. Popplet, https://itunes.apple.com/US/app/id374151636?mt=8.

18. http://popplet.com/

19. SimpleMind Free Mind Mapping, https://play.google.com/store/apps/details?id=com.modelmakertools.simplemindfree&hl=en.

20. Andrew Maka, "The Top Five Mind Mapping Apps for the Android Tablet," TechRepublic, July 20, 2012, http://www.techrepublic.com/blog/tablets-in-the-enterprise/the-top-five-mind-mapping-apps-for-the-android-tablet/.

21. http://www.scoop.it/ and http://paper.li/

22. https://hangouts.google.com/

23. Follow me on Twitter, https://twitter.com/nic221.

24. Buffer, https://buffer.com, and Hootsuite, https://hootsuite.com/ are both good services for scheduling your social media updates.

25. Mobile Apps News, http://nicolehennig.com/mobile-apps-news/.

26. Here's what one subscriber said: "Your app newsletter is awesome, I'd been extremely busy lately and couldn't check on news, but this newsletter precisely gave me what I wanted. Looking forward to your next issue. You are awesome!" Parikshit Joshi, http://nicolehennig.com/mobile-apps-news/.

27. https://mailchimp.com/

28. https://www.constantcontact.com

29. https://tinyletter.com/

30. https://www.pinterest.com/nic221/content-creation-with-mobile-apps/

31. https://www.pinterest.com/nic221/mobile-apps-for-education/

32. https://www.pinterest.com/nic221/infographics/

33. http://www.scoop.it/

34. ALA ecourses, http://ecourses.ala.org/course/index.php.

35. NEFLIN (Northeast Florida Library Information Network), for example, http://neflin.org/training/.

36. https://www.udemy.com and https://teachable.com/

37. My courses: http://nicolehennig.com/courses/.

38. My course, "Apps for Librarians," has an on-demand version on Udemy. https://www.udemy.com/apps4librarians/?couponCode=HENNIG2.

39. https://www.webex.com/

40. https://www.gotomeeting.com/

41. http://www.adobe.com/products/adobeconnect.html

42. See my complete list of webinars, http://nicolehennig.com/webinars/.

43. https://teachable.com/

44. Sakunthala, "High Tech Cool Hunting," Software Is Eating the World, March 11, 2016, https://medium.com/software-is-eating-the-world/high-tech -coolhunting-8b55879ea436#.df6dddy0x.

45. Satoshi Nakamoto, "Bitcoin: A Peer-to-Peer Electronic Cash System," Whitepaper on Bitcoin.org, 2008, https://bitcoin.org/bitcoin.pdf.

46. Don Tapscott and Alex Tapscott, "Here's Why Blockchains Will Change the World," Fortune, May 8, 2016, http://fortune.com/2016/05/08/why-blockchains -will-change-the-world/.

47. Nathaniel Popper, "A Bitcoin Believer's Crisis of Faith," New York Times, January 14, 2016, http://www.nytimes.com/2016/01/17/business/dealbook/the -bitcoin-believer-who-gave-up.html.

48. https://www.kickstarter.com/

49. https://slack.com/

50. https://www.reddit.com/

51. This is according to the ideas found in Everett M. Rogers book, *Diffusion of Innovations,* New York: Free Press, 5th edition, 2005. See also "Diffusion of Innovations Theory," University of Oklahoma Department of Communication, accessed December 6, 2016, http://www.ou.edu/deptcomm/dodjcc/groups/99A2/ theories.htm.

52. For example, Boston Virtual Reality Meetup, https://www.meetup.com/ Boston-Virtual-Reality/.

53. http://stackoverflow.com/

54. https://news.ycombinator.com/

55. Sakunthala, "High Tech Cool Hunting," Software is Eating the World, March 11, 2016, https://medium.com/software-is-eating-the-world/high-tech -coolhunting-8b55879ea436#.df6dddy0x.

56. https://www.technologyreview.com/lists/technologies/2016/

57. http://kk.org/about-me

58. http://kk.org/books/the-inevitable/

59. Elise Moreau, "The Rise of the Animated GIF: How GIFs Are Taking over Social Media & Influencing Online Photojournalism," Lifewire, October 19, 2016, https://www.lifewire.com/rise-of-animated-gif-3485813.

60. http://www.urbandictionary.com/define.php?term=doxing

61. The Next News Network, "LED Screen Rolls up like Paper," YouTube video, July 11, 3014, https://www.youtube.com/watch?v=RcomiyOFK4k.

62. "Suzhou Sky Screen," accessed December 6, 2016, http://www.electrosonic.com/middle-east/middle-east/projects/suzhou-sky-screen.

63. "A Computational Model of Knitting," k2g2 blog, accessed December 6, 2016, http://www.k2g2.org/blog:bit.craft:computational_model_of_knitting.

64. Benita Matofska, "What Is the Sharing Economy?," The People Who Share, September 1, 2016, http://www.thepeoplewhoshare.com/blog/what-is-the-sharing-economy/.

65. James Altucher podcast, "Ep. 173 – Kevin Kelly: One Rule for Predicting What You Never Saw Coming. . .," June 28, 2016, http://www.jamesaltucher.com/2016/06/kevinkelly/.

CHAPTER 7

Experimenting

Hands-On Play

Now that you've been learning about new technologies and coming up with ideas for how they could meet user needs, you'll need to get some hands-on experience.

Creating opportunities for you and your staff to test new technologies is important. You've very likely heard of the idea of a "technology petting zoo," where libraries make some new devices available to users and staff so they can try them out. For example, many libraries have offered loanable e-readers and tablets of different types, especially when these devices were new. It's important for your staff to have a chance to try out hardware, gadgets, software, and apps.[1]

In our user experience department at the MIT Libraries, we had a small budget for trying out new gadgets. This gave us a chance to try new devices before our users began to ask questions about them and also gave us a chance to figure out which of them might be best for use in dedicated programs and services. In order to try out apps, we purchased iTunes gift cards so that our staff members (five of us) could purchase some apps to put on their iPads. (When iPads were new, each of the five user experience staff received one.) Later we set up a program where anyone from our entire staff could borrow new iPad or Android tablets from our department. That way more people would have a chance to experience these firsthand.

It's a good idea to provide ways for a small number of your staff to be on the forefront of testing new gadgets, devices, apps, and services. The fact that hands-on play is a vital part of learning is something that most people can understand (even naysayers). It's also a good way to figure out which new technologies *aren't* worth using for more dedicated programs. And it's a good way to learn which details you will need to create policies for.

Framing this kind of thing as "hands-on play" is a good idea. When you've heard the phrase, "but how will we support this?" many times, this is a way to try new technologies without knowing yet how you will support them. Both staff and users can be part of these experiments, and you can get good feedback from your users about which technologies might matter most to them. Having a special name for this kind of experiment helps, whether it's a "petting zoo" or some other creative name.

If it's not gadgets you are testing, but software or apps, you'll need to be able to play with them thoroughly yourself before setting up experiments with users. Set aside time on a regular basis to test out new software, apps, and online services. Often free trials or free versions are available that can give you enough experience to learn the basics of what's possible. It's also useful to have a modest budget for testing out new software and apps in the same way as you're testing out gadgets and hardware.

After you've tested some new technologies in a hands-on way, you are ready to move to the stage of setting up small experiments with the most promising technologies. These experiments may last for several weeks or even a few months, with a plan for getting enough user feedback to decide whether to move them into a fully supported service offering. This is the topic of the next chapter.

Designing Experiments and Evaluating the Results

If you are working in the world of emerging technologies for libraries, I'm sure you are familiar with the resistance that people often feel about new technologies. You will find many books and articles written about how a particular technology is going to ruin people (especially children) and destroy civilization.[2]

You may have heard this statement about information overload from the Swiss scientist, Conrad Gessner: "The modern world overwhelms people with data. This overabundance is both 'confusing' and 'harmful' to the mind."[3] If you don't recognize his name, it might be because he died in 1565 and his warnings referred to the overwhelming amount of information unleashed by the printing press.

This has been going on throughout history, when new technologies appeared. I like this quote from Douglas Adams, the author of *The Hitchhiker's Guide to the Galaxy*:

"Anything that is in the world when you're born is normal and ordinary and is just a natural part of the way the world works. Anything that's invented between when you're fifteen and thirty-five is new and exciting and revolutionary and you can probably get a career in it. Anything invented after you're thirty-five is against the natural order of things."[4]

Someone who doesn't take that view is Kevin Kelly, the author of *The Inevitable: Understanding the 12 Technological Forces That Will Shape Our Future,* which I mentioned in the section on trends versus fads.

In his book, he advocates for the embracing of new technologies, experimenting with them, and facing the truth about the qualities of each new technology. It's only through trying and testing new technologies that we can learn what they are best used for. With that knowledge, we can "civilize" technologies and design the best laws and social norms around them.

This is a point of view that I agree with. As information professionals, we can design experiments that help us learn how particular technologies will most benefit our users and meet our strategic goals. It's useful to have a continual cycle of experiments that will give us solid information. We can use this information to make decisions based on real-world results, rather than having endless theoretical discussions.

Embrace new technologies rather than fight them. Accept them and work with them. We can mold them and make them work for us. It's not likely that new technologies that people think could be harmful will disappear, even if they are outlawed. Even printed books were a new technology that people feared at one time.

Create a Space for Experimentation

Between 2006 and 2011, Google Labs was a space where experiments with new technologies from Google were presented. They described it as "a playground where our more adventurous users can play around with prototypes of some of our wild and crazy ideas and offer feedback directly to the engineers who developed them."[5] At the MIT Libraries, we used that as a model for our website called "MIT Libraries Betas."[6] That has since evolved into a page called "Experiments at the MIT Libraries:" http://libraries.mit.edu/about/experiments/. Whatever you decide to call it, it's a good idea to have a special place online where you offer one or more experiments to your users.

Create a Place for What You Decide *Not* to Move Forward With

When you design an experiment, you'll need to create some criteria for what will make it a success, and I'll discuss that in the next section. For those items that you decide *not* to move forward with, you can make a special section telling users what you learned and why you decided not to offer it. At the MIT Libraries, we had a page called "The Betas Graveyard," where we listed those items[7] (the term "graveyard" was inspired by Google Labs).

Create a Place to List Experiments That Have Been Turned into Fully Supported Library Services

Once an experiment is over and you've decided to move it into a formally supported library service, you can list it in a special place on your experiments page. That way people can see what you've tried and which ones turned into something concrete.

We used the term "Graduates of Betas" for this, again inspired by Google Labs and their terminology. So to summarize, we listed "current betas, retired betas (in the betas graveyard), and graduates of betas."

Having special names for your experiments and a place to list the ones that "failed" and the ones that "succeeded" helps everyone to understand your process and see how hands-on experimentation is a great way to learn about new technologies.

Not Being Afraid to "Fail"

In order to do this kind of creative work, we need to make our culture one where people aren't afraid to fail. According to experts like Robert Sutton, who wrote *Weird Ideas That Work*,[8] "The most creative people ... have the greatest number of failures because they do the most stuff."[9] When you work in an atmosphere of perfectionism, it's hard to feel that you can take risks without being judged harshly.

So what makes people feel OK about taking risks in the workplace? A study done by Jim McCormick, an expert in performance improvement through intelligent risk-taking, found that people would take risks if they had two things: "assurances that less-than-ideal outcomes would not negatively affect their regard or career (49%), or clear direction and support from leadership to take risks (31%)."[10]

So what if, during performance reviews, you asked your staff to come prepared with a list of experiments they tried that didn't work out?

You could ask them to discuss what they learned from both successful and unsuccessful experiments. People need reassurance that they won't be judged for taking risks when setting up experiments with emerging technologies. For more thoughts on how to encourage this type of culture in your workplace, see "How to Encourage Successful Innovation," February 1, 2015, http://www.newandimproved.com/white-papers.aspx?newsid=569.

Designing Experiments

So how might you set up an experiment? Let's say that you want to test a new web browser widget that has the potential to be useful for your community. One example from several years ago was a new tool called LibX.[11] It's a browser toolbar that makes it easy to quickly search library resources from other pages on the web, such as the page for a book on Amazon. You're probably familiar with it, since it's been around for quite some time.

Here are some steps to keep in mind, no matter what technology you are testing.

1. **Alpha testing.** You and your own staff should thoroughly test the technology as a first step (alpha testing before beta testing with users). Make sure it works in different situations and locations, and if it's a web or mobile tool, test it on different platforms. For LibX, our staff tested it on different browsers and made sure we knew thoroughly how it worked.

2. **Create instructions for users.** This doesn't have to be long and wordy, just make sure you have a few tips for how to try the new technology and put them on your website or other place that makes sense for the technology in question. For LibX, we made a web page with instructions for downloading it, screenshots of how it worked, and we made a short screencast video of it as well.

3. **Determine your objectives.** Decide what you want to find out about it during your experiment. What problems are you trying to solve with it? Does it have any unexpected benefits that you didn't imagine? Which kinds of users would be most likely to find it useful? For LibX, we saw that it could be helpful for any of our library users, since we knew they spent a lot of time discovering resources on other websites than our own. This would make it easy for them to quickly search our catalog and databases right from those other sites. We wanted to know if they found it convenient and if it saved them time and frustration.

4. **Get feedback.** You might want to set up a simple feedback form so your users can comment on the tool. Alternatively you could provide a special e-mail address for people to write to. At the MIT Libraries, we had a special e-mail list that went to a small group of staff in our user experience department so that frontline librarians who didn't have a chance to learn about an experimental technology yet could direct questions to us. We used one e-mail address for all of our experiments.

5. **Document what happens.** Keep track of all feedback and questions that your users have. Keep a count of how many people tested it (or downloaded it, if it's downloadable). You'll need both kinds of data (quantitative and qualitative) when it's time to persuade decision-makers that your experiment should be turned into a supported service. If it makes sense, you might want to observe people using it (with their permission), especially if it involves new hardware to be used in the library. If it makes sense (and with permission), take some photos of people using it because this will be helpful later when you are making the case to use it as a library service. If that's not possible, you could take photos of you and your own staff using it. This can be useful if it's a technology that will require some visual explanation when you are explaining it to others on your staff who aren't familiar with it. For LibX, we didn't need photos, we just recorded what people said on the feedback form and in any e-mails they sent to us. We also kept statistics on how many people downloaded and installed it.

6. **Publicize it.** Create a special place on your website to post information about any experiments you are running. You can add instructions, tell people how to test it, link to feedback forms, and offer a disclaimer about how it's not fully supported, since it's only an experiment.

7. **Schedule a time to evaluate it.** Decide when to evaluate the experiment. We most often used the end of each academic semester to review our experiments and decide which to "graveyard" and which to "graduate." You can decide what kind of schedule makes sense for the experiments you are working on. We found it useful to group them by semester, but you may find different time periods make sense, depending on the scope of your experiments.

Evaluating the Results of Your Experiments

In order to decide whether each of your experiments should move forward into a supported service, you'll need to develop criteria for success. The next section will discuss some ideas for criteria that you might use.

Criteria for Evaluating Your Experiments

It's useful to come up with a list of criteria at the start for "graduating" your experiments into a library service. Look at everything from user impact, to staff impact, to your library's strategic goals.

Here is what we used at the MIT Libraries. To graduate, an experiment did not have to meet all of these criteria. These mainly served as a framework for our discussion at the end of each experiment.

Criteria for Graduating from an Experiment to a Supported Service

A. User impact
- solves a known problem
- affects a large number of users
- shows that we're on the cutting edge
- it's fun (for us and for our users)
- it's been requested by multiple users

B. Helps meet our goals
- improves known-item searching
- improves topical discovery
- improves connections with other systems and tools
- helps with evaluating best sources of information
- helps users save time helps with personal information management (saving, sorting, sharing, citing what they found)

C. Staff impact
- It doesn't take a huge amount of staff time to implement.
- It's something that we already know how to do or could easily find out how to do.
- It's something we could delegate to students, interns, or temporary help.
- It's something that doesn't cost a great deal of extra money to implement.
- It improves staff workflow and saves time.
- It solves more than one problem with one solution.

Remember, each technology did not have to meet all of these criteria. Instead we looked for technologies that were easy to support with existing resources and also had clear value for our users.

You'll notice that we included some subjective items, such as "it's fun," or "it shows we're on the cutting edge." Most of that language was internal to our team who created and evaluated the experiments and might not fly with people you are asking to make your projects a priority. Of course being at MIT, we especially wanted to be "on the cutting edge," and like any library we ran up against lack of funding or lack of priorities for the services we were proposing. But the value of having fun with technology is a strong one, especially at MIT, so we included it in our criteria.

Decide What to "Graveyard"

When deciding which technologies *not* to move forward with, we considered the following:

- There is no easy way to support it.
- It's still too breakable—not ready for prime time.
- It's been superseded by another tool that does the same thing better.
- There is unproven user need for the service.

And on our web page for users where we listed the experiments we had discontinued, we said this:

> While many beta tools and services of the MIT Libraries are great successes, others haven't been as fruitful. Some criteria that we use to take a beta out of service include:

- No way to support it
- Superseded by another tool or service
- Unproven user need for the service

> As Henry Ford said, "Failure is only the opportunity to begin again more intelligently." We've learned something from each of the tools that we've tried and have used the knowledge in planning future services.[12]

We wanted to be public about our experiments with our students and faculty, who were usually quite interested in what we were experimenting with and more than willing to give their feedback.

You can make a similar list of criteria and tell your users what you are experimenting with. In addition, it's always good to show to those who are managing and funding your library that you are being selective and smart about new technologies that you are implementing as fully supported services.

User Impact

Now is a good time to go back and look at the results of any information you have about your users. Look at survey results, user needs studies, interviews, focus groups, and field studies. See the section on gathering information about user needs earlier in this book. If you don't have results from specific studies you've carried out, you can often find useful information from published studies done by other institutions similar to yours.[13]

Look for specific known problems that your proposed new technology services can help solve. When you tie your proposed services to specific user needs, it will help you make a case that your new project should be given time and funding.

Help Meet Your Library's Goals

The goals that you use will be specific to your library. Most libraries have a strategic plan, and it's good to look at yours so you can line up your experiments with your institution's stated goals. This comes in very handy later when you are presenting to decision-makers who will approve your project.

At the time of these experiments, our strategic plan[14] had some priorities in it, such as:

- Advance digital scholarship and research.
- Expand investments in digital content management infrastructure and services.
- Participate actively in digital learning at MIT.
- Enhance the on-campus experience through transformed library services and spaces.
- Strengthen support for MIT's global engagement.

So when any of our newly proposed services fit clearly into one of these priorities, that helped it get funded. You might notice that these goals are quite broad. The items we listed in the criteria above under "helps meet our goals" were focused on more specific goals that we had as a department. Sometimes it's useful to drill down into the goals of your department if you are in a large institution.

For public libraries, take a look at the Seattle Public Library's strategic plan for an example of some goals.[15]

- Fuel Seattle's Passion for Reading, Personal Growth & Learning
- Expand Seattle's Access to Information, Ideas & Stories

- Empower Seattle's Distinctive Communities & Vibrant Neighborhoods
- Build Partnerships to Make a Difference in People's Lives
- Foster an Organizational Culture of Innovation

The last goal about fostering a culture of innovation is common to the strategic goals of many libraries, and by experimenting that's exactly what you are doing. So look for these documents from your library in order to help build your case.

Staff Impact

This is usually one of the most difficult areas to deal with. Many libraries are short-staffed and can't handle supporting one more service, especially if it requires technical knowledge that would require special training for your staff. You can see from our list above that we were looking for small wins, items that would be easy to implement, without needing a huge, highly trained staff to support. This doesn't mean that you might not sometimes be proposing a larger project, but often you can find small projects that make a huge difference to users without putting a huge strain on your staff.

An example of this would be the experiments we did with the LibX toolbar mentioned earlier. It was easy to support with existing staff resources, and it worked to make library research much more convenient for our users. The fact that users cared about convenience above all was one of the main themes we noticed in our user needs studies.[16]

Summary

As you can see, coming up with your list of criteria will help you decide which experiments are worth proposing as supported library services. In the next chapter, we'll look at how to present your results in order to persuade decision-makers who control your time and budgets.

But before we do that, let's look at a methodology that will help you define user problems and come up with creative solutions using new technologies. Putting your experiments into a framework like the one is very useful. That methodology is called "design thinking."

Project Methods: Design Thinking

The most useful framework I've found for bringing new technologies to fruition within a library is the process called "design thinking."[17] Design thinking is an approach that helps you design solutions to problems you've identified that your users experience. It comes from the field of visual design and can be applied to other fields as a process for solving problems. It looks at the overlap between three areas: desirability (meeting user needs), financial viability, and technological feasibility. Where these three aspects overlap is where innovation happens.

It's called "design thinking" because it comes from the practices that designers use to solve problems. It's a point of view that sees problems as opportunities and helps lead you toward solutions that can transform a product or service. It involves being creative in the face of ambiguity and working within whatever constraints you have (time, money, or staffing).

This process involves three overlapping phases:

- Inspiration—define your challenge
- Ideation—generate ideas
- Iteration—experiment in cycles

Inspiration is about defining your design challenge and looking at new perspectives on it. Ideation is about generating ideas and making those ideas tangible. Iteration is about creating cycles of experimentation, based on the feedback of your users.

This approach is useful for libraries because it is patron-centered. It's based on learning by doing and it's experimental. The mind-set used for this approach is about looking at the world through a beginner's eyes, being confident in spite of setbacks and failures, and seeing problems as opportunities. It's an optimistic outlook.

It's very different than a linear approach where you write a complete project plan, with a timeline and all the details in place. That type of planning is appropriate for big implementation projects, but this one is better for solving specific user problems and discovering the best possible uses of emerging technologies for library users.

Design Challenge

To begin a design thinking project, you first need to come up with a design challenge. The recommended way to do this is to use "how might we" questions. Think of something you've been wanting to change in your library and come up with a list of "how might we" questions about it. For example, "How might we work more effectively with those whose first language isn't English?" or "How might we better teach information literacy skills?"[18]

Inspiration

The inspiration stage has to do with getting new perspectives from your users. During this stage, you might interview a few individual users about not only the specific challenge but also about their lives and goals. Another method would be to immerse yourself in the world of your users. For example, if your challenge involves blind users, try to perform certain simple tasks while blindfolded. And yet another method would be to visit unexpected places, such as museums (if you're working on displays for the library), or busy coffee shops where people study (if you're working on study spaces). All of these methods will give you some inspiration for seeing the problem from different perspectives.

Ideation

This phase involves generating lots of new ideas that might serve as solutions. Use different types of brainstorming methods to approach idea generation with your team. The best methods include the following practices: defer judgment, encourage wild ideas, build on ideas that other people have, stay focused on the topic, be visual, and go for quantity.

Going for quantity is a practice where you might set a crazy goal, like to come up with 50 ideas in 10 minutes. The advantage of this is that after running out of "normal" ideas, people start to come up with truly innovative solutions. I'll discuss more ideation methods in the next chapter, along with some examples.

Building Prototypes

Next you'll need to choose a few favorite ideas and try to bring them to life by building prototypes. This can help you work out some of the concrete details and see what may or may not work. It's a way to get ideas out of your head and into the world, where other people can react to it.

Prototypes can be made in different ways—using paper, cardboard, craft supplies, pens and markers, fabrics, tools, and so on. They could be a model of something physical (such as a special type of workstation for a new technology), a digital mock-up (such as screens of a mobile app), or a role-play (such as acting out how an in-person or online interactive service would work).

Iteration

You can show these prototypes to your colleagues and your users in order to get feedback on their feasibility and how they might be improved. You only need a handful of people to get useful feedback. You may want to start with people you know are friends of your library. Be sure to ask for their honest, critical, constructive feedback in addition to positive feedback.

You could ask questions like these:

- Can you describe what excites you the most about this idea, and why?
- If you could change one thing about this prototype, what would it be?
- What would you like to improve about this idea?
- What do you not like about this idea?[19]

The next step is to look at all your answers and think about both the positive feedback and what could be improved. You can use this information to come up with some new iterations of your idea. Keep a list of what new questions you would like to explore with the next iteration.

After you prototype several iterations, you'll have some valuable information. You could decide on any of these as next steps:

- Build a team to develop the idea further until a specific date.
- Ask for more funding or resources based on your prototypes so far.
- Set aside time on your own to keep developing your idea.

Getting to Scale

The final part of the design thinking process is about finding a way to bring your idea to fruition. Here is where you tell the story of your work and make a pitch for the resources you need to make it happen. It's a good idea to document your process of learning about your users and their feedback on your prototypes—take photos, get permission to use them, and take lots of notes. You can tell a persuasive story with this documentation, and you'll need to do that to persuade those who will approve and fund it. This part of the process I'll discuss further in an upcoming chapter of this book.

Summary

This is just a high level overview of design thinking. There are many more useful details and examples to help you learn this method.

To use this process, I recommend downloading the following free toolkit, "Design Thinking for Libraries: A Toolkit for Patron-Centered Design," http://designthinkingforlibraries.com/. This toolkit came out of a project funded by the Bill & Melinda Gates Foundation and led by the firm IDEO in 2013–2014. They partnered with librarians from the Chicago Public Library in the United States and the Aarhus Public Libraries in Denmark. They also observed more than 40 librarians from 10 countries and used what they learned from their experiments in creating this toolkit.

Another useful resource is "Design Thinking for Educators," created by IDEO in conjunction with K-12 educators, http://www.design thinkingforeducators.com/.

Project Methods: Agile and "The Lean Startup"

Another methodology that you hear mentioned often these days is "agile." It's a method for developing software that was created by a group of developers who met in 2001 to find common ground on how to develop software more effectively. What came from that meeting was a "Manifesto for Agile Software Development."[20]

It came out of a desire to break away from some of the baggage of corporate environments where in a "Dilbert-[21]like" fashion decision-makers were making demands of developers that didn't make sense. A practice known as the "waterfall model" that was appropriate for developing hardware turned out not to make sense for software development. With the waterfall model, you make a complete project plan with a timeline and documentation in advance and don't release the project until everything is done and as close to perfect as possible. It's called "waterfall" because the process flows downward "through the phases of conception, initiation, analysis, design, construction, testing, production/implementation, and maintenance."[22]

Agile is based on the following values (emphasis mine):

- **Individuals and interactions** over processes and tools
- **Working software** over comprehensive documentation
- **Customer collaboration** over contract negotiation
- **Responding to change** over following a plan
  (From http://agilemanifesto.org/)

It embraces the notion of perpetual beta—software should be made available as early as possible to get real-world feedback from users. And it should go through a continuous cycle of changes and improvements based on that feedback.

This is similar to the iteration part of the design thinking methodology. Here are a few of the principles, quoted directly from the manifesto.[23]

> Our highest priority is to satisfy the customer through early and continuous delivery of valuable software.
>
> Welcome changing requirements, even late in development. Agile processes harness change for the customer's competitive advantage.
>
> Deliver working software frequently, from a couple of weeks to a couple of months, with a preference to the shorter timescale.
>
> Build projects around motivated individuals. Give them the environment and support they need, and trust them to get the job done.
>
> Continuous attention to technical excellence and good design enhances agility.
>
> Simplicity—the art of maximizing the amount of work not done—is essential.
>
> At regular intervals, the team reflects on how to become more effective, then tunes and adjusts its behavior accordingly.

To read the full manifesto, see "Agile 'Software Development' Manifesto," http://agilemanifesto.org/principles.html.

I believe that agile methodology is an excellent idea for the implementation of new technology projects. It makes sense when you are developing new software or a new app.

Design thinking, on the other hand, is a useful methodology for solving user problems and developing new services in a library (whether software is involved or not).[24] It's an overall process for improving library services in a cyclical manner.

The Lean Startup

At some point you may have heard the term "minimum viable product" or MVP. This comes from an approach known as "The Lean Startup." It's a method developed by Eric Ries and described in his book of the same name, published in 2011.[25] It's an approach meant to help new startups get feedback early in their process of building a new product so that they can find out whether their idea is something that customers want and need. Without this process, startups have been known to develop something for many months without showing it to customers, later finding out that it's a flop because people don't want or need it.

The idea of "minimum viable product" is that a version of a new product should be put into customers' hands as early as possible so that the developers can collect a maximum amount of validated learning about customers.[26] When you start small and get something into the hands of a few real users as soon as possible, you can learn from their experience with it, to create something that solves real-world problems.

Sometimes a new product turns out to be not what people really want and need, but some aspect of it is actually more valuable and important to end users. When a project team changes direction based on user feedback, this is called a "pivot."[27]

An example of this happened when the photo-sharing service Flickr was first invented. It began as an online role-playing game. When the developers realized that their small feature of sharing photos within the game was what mattered most to users, they scrapped the game and focused on building the photo-sharing service, which became Flickr.[28] Some other interesting examples of pivots are (1) Yelp, which began as an automated system for e-mailing recommendation requests to friends, (2) YouTube, which began as a video-dating site called "Tune in Hook Up," and (3) PayPal, which originated as a way to exchange money via Palm Pilots.[29]

To learn more about the concept of pivoting, see "Top 10 Ways Entrepreneurs Pivot a Lean Startup" by Martin Zwilling in *Forbes*, September 16, 2011, http://www.forbes.com/sites/martinzwilling/2011/09/16/top-10-ways-entrepreneurs-pivot-a-lean-startup.

This advice for startups and entrepreneurs can be applied when developing new library products and services. Get a minimum viable version of your new service into peoples' hands, get feedback, and make decisions based on that. It can save a lot of time because you won't end up developing something that people don't need or want. And you can put your resources into the services that are the most valuable to your users.

Summary

Agile and "the lean startup" are both good methods to use when building new products or services. These methods are similar to design thinking because they focus on cycles that include user feedback. They are great methods to use when you begin to implement a new product or service, especially involving new technologies.

Design thinking, on the other hand, is most useful as the overall process for coming up with solutions to user problems and generating ideas for solving them—often using new and emerging technologies.

Ideation Methods

An important part of the design thinking process is the ideation stage. Coming up with creative and useful ideas for using new technologies is essential, no matter what process you are using.

Many experts talk about the importance of coming up with a large quantity of ideas in order to come up with the best ideas. The molecular biologist Linus Pauling once said, "If you want to have good ideas you must have many ideas. Most of them will be wrong, and what you have to learn is which ones to throw away."[30] In this section we'll focus on generating many ideas and later we'll look at how to throw out the bad ones.

There are two books in particular that are useful for finding techniques beyond traditional brainstorming. Each of these books is a catalog of methods, with the purpose and a description for each technique. When I worked for the MIT Libraries, our user experience department staff used several of these techniques to help us come up with good ideas.

The books are *Thinkertoys: A Handbook of Creative Thinking Techniques* by Michael Michalko and *Gamestorming: A Playbook for Innovators, Rulebreakers, and Changemakers* by Dave Gray.[31] There is also a useful card deck by Michael Michalko, called *Thinkpak: A Brainstorming Card Deck*.[32] It's a handy way to use these techniques, since one activity from the book is printed on each card.

Here are a few examples of exercises to help you come up with ideas for using emerging technologies for innovative library services.

1. Brainwriting[33]

This exercise is best for a small group of 5 to 10 people. To begin, you define a problem and write it in a place visible to everyone. Using a "how might we" question (as described in the "design thinking" section) is a good idea.

Distribute a few index cards to each person in your group and ask them to silently come up with ideas that answer that question. No idea is too wild or crazy. Let them know that this is a silent exercise.

After they write an idea on a card, they pass the card to the person on their right. Give people time to quietly think of ideas and write them on individual cards. When they receive a card from the person on their left, they are instructed to use it as a spark to ignite a related or enhanced version of the idea and write it on the same card. After a few minutes, people are thinking and writing and reacting to cards, sometimes passing them on, sometimes adding ideas to the same idea posed by another. Keep going until you have multiple ideas on each card.

When you're finished, collect the cards and attach them to the board around the central question. Then have the group come up to the board and read the ideas to themselves, putting a star on the ones they find most compelling. Then have a group discussion about the starred ideas.

This method has two benefits. First, it gives everyone time to think and contribute ideas equally (including introverts who may not get their ideas heard in a room full of extroverts). Secondly, since most of the ideas will be cocreated, there is more of a chance of follow-through because multiple people feel ownership of the idea.

We did this several times at various stages of ideation for projects we were working on in our user experience group, with our team feeling quite positive about this method compared to traditional brainstorming.

2. Worst Idea[34]

This method is something I enjoyed participating in with a small group at a user experience workshop I attended.[35] It's also described in more than one creativity book, including this one: *Idea Stormers: How to Lead and Inspire Creative Breakthroughs.*[36]

For this idea, ask your group to come up with a list of terrible, stupid, and possibly illegal ideas in response to your problem. Alternatively, ask them to describe the worst possible version of a particular library service that you want to improve—anything from your physical spaces to online services. This usually gets people laughing and joking, since it's pretty easy to come up with bad ideas.

Do this out loud with a small group and write everything on the board or on flip charts. When you've run out of ideas, the next step is to go through each bad idea and reverse it. You might be able to reverse it in more than one way. Usually some of the reversals will be really good ideas about how to improve the service.

Here's an example that's not related to libraries but was used at the workshop I attended, since it's an easy topic for people to discuss.

The question was, how could you design the worst possible airport? This is something most people can relate to.

For example, in the worst airport there might be no chairs or seating of any kind. It might be too hot or too cold. It might be very large with no way to get from one terminal to another other than walking. There might be no food available or allowed. There might be only the most unhealthy and stale junk food available. There might be no outlets for charging your mobile devices.

You could go on and on with this. But it's where the reversals happen that good ideas come up. For example, the opposite of no outlets would be to have outlets at every seat. And to offer special charging stations with different types of cables available. For the seating problem, you could have more seats in the areas that need it most and even offer special reclining seats for taking naps (as you see in some international airports). Of course, many of these solutions are already in some airports.

The benefits of this method are that people enjoy this approach and end up laughing and relaxing (leading to more creative ideas). It's good to use when you aren't having good luck with other methods or when people feel pressured to come up with perfect or great ideas. This method breaks through that in a fun way.

3. Lotus Blossom Diagram[37]

The Lotus Blossom Diagram method[38] was invented by Yasuo Matsumura of Clover Management Research in Chiba City, Japan.[39] It's a method that helps you look at the big picture and many of the surrounding issues of a particular problem or challenge. It helps you to generate a large number of ideas in a systematic way.

For this method you need to print a large square divided into 64 squares, 9 rows, and 9 columns. See the illustration here for an example: http://5by5 design.com/blog/design-practice/lotus-blossom-technique/. Another example can be found here: http://thoughtegg.com/lotus-blossom -creative-technique/.

Eight 3 × 3 squares (known as blossoms) are arranged around the central set of squares (central blossom). You can make a printed or digital version of this chart using a spreadsheet. It's usually nice to print a very large version for a group to work with. We printed one the size of a flip-chart page.

Add the letters *A* through *H* in each square around the center square. Also put the each letter in the center of each group of nine squares surrounding the central group.

In the center box, labeled "I," you write down your challenge or problem to be explored. As in previous exercises, it's useful to pose the question as "how might we." In each of the adjacent boxes (A through H), you list related aspects of the problem.

Each of those subproblems then becomes the center of a new blossom. For example, take what's in box A and write it again in the center of the upper left blossom. Then use the squares surrounding that to write possible solutions to that aspect of the problem. Do this for each of the eight aspects (A through H).

As you can see, this might take some time and could perhaps be completed over several meetings. One way to come up with the first list of A through H subtopics is to consider your problem to be the topic of a book, and each of those is a chapter.

Your goal with each of the blossoms is to come up with eight ideas for solving that subproblem. To see an example of this method that we used at the MIT Libraries, see my photo set on Flickr: https://www.flickr.com/photos/nic221/albums/72157624129345469/with/4688609209/. This was used when our user experience department was brand new, with a staff of about five librarians. Since we were a new department, we needed to come up with some creative ways to achieve our goals. Our central problem as stated was, "how can we help our staff develop empathy for our users?" Perhaps a better version of that statement would have been "how might we help our staff see library services from the users' point of view?" See the whole chart, in progress here: https://www.flickr.com/photos/nic221/4688629125/sizes/l.

As you can see, eventually you will end up with 64 ideas, each set of ideas addressing a subproblem. You may not use all of these ideas, but the sheer volume of ideas usually turns up some good ones.

One of the ideas that came out of this for us was a small project we did with our library staff in 2010 called, "Patron for a Day," which I described in Chapter 4 of this book.

For more ideas and example of the Lotus Blossom Technique, see "The Lotus Blossom Creative Technique" by Robert Riley on a blog called *Thought Egg*: http://thoughtegg.com/lotus-blossom-creative-technique/.

4. What If Libraries Were Like ...?

In this exercise, you find positive examples of products or services outside of the world of libraries, and then ask, "What if libraries were like [the product]?" It's a way to combine ideas from different fields to come up with creative solutions.

To do this exercise divide into small groups and give each group some information about a product or service that delights users. It could be a retail product and should be outside of the world of libraries. Then ask each group to come up with multiple answers to, "What if libraries were like [the product]?" For example, "What if libraries were like Zipcar?"

Back in 2009, we did this exercise using the Good Brands Report from PSFK.[40] This report from the consulting firm PSFK discusses brands in terms of their innovation, good design, sense of community with users, environmental benefits, and more.

Some of the brands discussed in this free report included Apple, Zipcar, Twitter, IKEA, and Skype. For example, Zipcar was discussed in terms of offering a service instead of a product (a new idea at that time).

The report was handy because it had a one-page description of what delighted customers from that brand and why. Each of our groups were given a page from this report that described an innovative brand. They used that to help spark their discussion.

If you don't have access to a particular report like this, you can choose well-known products or services that everyone is familiar with. When you look at the aspects of a product or service that delight people and apply those aspects to library services, many creative ideas spring up.

Summary

As you can see, there are many techniques available for generating lots of creative ideas. The two books mentioned previously (*Thinkertoys* and *Gamestorming*) are excellent sources for these techniques and are worth using for many projects. You might be wondering how to narrow down these large lists of ideas and how to decide which ones might best meet the needs of your users while still being practical and cost-effective to implement. For that, use the techniques in the first few sections of this chapter: hands-on play, designing experiments, and developing criteria for evaluating your experiments.

For a concrete example of how this could work in a library, read the report I mentioned earlier: "Design Thinking for Libraries: A Toolkit for Patron-Centered Design," http://designthinkingforlibraries.com/.

After you've got some specific ideas for using a new technology in your library (backed by the results of your experiments and evaluated according to the criteria you've developed), you're ready to move toward implementation—the topic of the next chapter.

Endnotes

1. "Gadget Petting Zoos: Tips & Success Stories," March 15, 2013, http://ides.winnefox.org/gadget-petting-zoo.

2. For example, see this review of *The Shallows: What the Internet Is Doing to Our Brains,* by Nicholas Carr: Jonah Lehrer, "Our Cluttered Minds," *New York Times*, June 3, 2010, http://www.nytimes.com/2010/06/06/books/review/Lehrer-t.html. See also this review of *The Cult of the Amateur: How Today's Internet Is Killing Our Culture,* by Andrew Keen: "YouTube If You Want to ... The Internet Is Overrated and Even Harmful According to Andrew Keen's The Culture of the Amateur," *The Guardian,* July 7, 2007, https://www.theguardian.com/books/2007/jul/08/computingandthenet.society.

3. Vaughan Bell, "Don't Touch That Dial!, A History of Media Technology Scares, from the Printing Press to Facebook," *Slate*, February 15, 2010, http://www.slate.com/articles/health_and_science/science/2010/02/dont_touch_that_dial.single.html.

4. Douglas Adams, *The Salmon of Doubt: Hitchhiking the Galaxy One Last Time* (London: Macmillan, 2002), http://www.worldcat.org/oclc/59407526.

5. "Google Labs FAQ," archived from the original, accessed December 6, 2016, https://web.archive.org/web/20110726095055/http:/www.googlelabs.com/faq#whatis.

6. You can see an archived version of our betas page in Internet Archive, http://web.archive.org/web/20100601191240/http:/libraries.mit.edu/help/betas/.

7. See an archived version of our "Betas Graveyard," http://web.archive.org/web/20100610035707/http:/libraries.mit.edu/help/betas/graveyard.html.

8. Robert Sutton, *Weird Ideas That Work: How to Build a Creative Company* (New York: Free Press, 2007).

9. Robert Sutton, "Reward Success and Failure, Punish Inaction," *Bob Sutton: Work Matters*, February 10, 2009, http://bobsutton.typepad.com/my_weblog/2009/02/reward-success-and-failure-punish-inaction.html.

10. Jim McCormick, "Seeking Initiative and Innovation? Reward Failure!" *SelfGrowth.com*, accessed December 6, 2016, http://www.selfgrowth.com/articles/Seeking_Initiative_and_Innovation_Reward_Failure.html.

11. http://libx.org/

12. See an archived version of the page: http://web.archive.org/web/20100610035707/http:/libraries.mit.edu/help/betas/graveyard.html.

13. Studies like these: Nancy Fried Foster, *Studying Students: A Second Look* (Chicago: ACRL, 2013), and Nancy Fried Foster and Susan Gibbons, eds., *Studying Students: The Undergraduate Research Project at the University of Rochester* (Chicago: ACRL, 2007). A free copy is available here: http://www.ala.org/acrl/sites/ala.org.acrl/files/content/publications/booksanddigitalresources/digital/Foster-Gibbons_cmpd.pdf.

14. "MIT Libraries Strategic Plan, 2014-2016," accessed December 6, 2016, https://libraries.mit.edu/wp-content/uploads/2014/01/strategic_plan_2014-2016.pdf

15. Seattle Public Library, *My Library: The Next Generation, The Seattle Public Library Strategic Plan,* adopted February 23, 2011, https://www.spl.org/Documents/about/strategic_plan.pdf.

16. "2011 Digital Scholarship Study: An Executive Summary," MIT Libraries User Experience Group, October 2011, http://hennigweb.com/keeping-up/dig-scholarship-summary.pdf.

17. IDEO, "Design Thinking for Libraries: A Toolkit for Patron Centered Design," December 31, 2014, http://designthinkingforlibraries.com/.

18. To see a list of "how might we" questions we used at the MIT Libraries, see https://wikis.mit.edu/confluence/pages/viewpage.action?pageId=78434571.

19. Questions from "Design Thinking in a Day," *Libraries Toolkit at a Glance,* p. 14, free PDF download: http://www.designthinkingforlibraries.com/.

20. http://agilemanifesto.org/

21. Dilbert is the comic strip by Scott Adams that makes fun of corporate workplaces and clueless bosses http://dilbert.com/.

22. Hari Thapliyal, "Agile vs Waterfall Project Management, Rare Mentors," August 29, 2016, http://rarementors.com/lms/agile-vs-waterfall-project-management/.]

23. "Principles of Agile Software Development," accessed December 6, 2016, http://agilemanifesto.org/principles.html.

24. For more about the differences, see Matt Cooper-Wright, "The Blurring between Design Thinking and Agile," *Front-Line Interaction Design*, November 23, 2016, https://medium.com/front-line-interaction-design/the-blurring-between-design-thinking-and-agile-ae59d14f28e3#.bp5hrxn8e.

25. Eric Ries, *The Lean Startup : How Today's Entrepreneurs Use Continuous Innovation to Create Radically Successful Businesses* (New York : Crown Business, 2011).

26. Eric Ries, "Minimum Viable Product: A Guide," *Startup Lessons Learned,* August 3, 2009,http://www.startuplessonslearned.com/2009/08/minimum-viable-product-guide.html and "Validated Learning about Customers," April 14, 2009, http://www.startuplessonslearned.com/2009/04/validated-learning-about-customers.html.

27. Suren Samarchyan, "How Do You Define a Pivot in Product Development?" *Quora*, September 6, 2014, https://www.quora.com/How-do-you-define-a-pivot-in-Product-development.

28. Jefferson Graham, "Flickr of Idea on a Gaming Project Led to Photo Website," *USA Today,* February 27, 2006, http://usatoday30.usatoday.com/tech/products/2006-02-27-flickr_x.htm.

29. Nicholas Thomas, "11 Startups That Found Success By Changing Direction," *Mashable*, July 8, 2011, http://mashable.com/2011/07/08/startups-change-direction/#9J0ewwk5rPqm.

30. Francis Crick, "The Impact of Linus Pauling on Molecular Biology," The Pauling Symposium, Oregon State University, Special Collections, Oregon State University Libraries, 1996, http://oregonstate.edu/dept/Special_Collections/subpages/ahp/1995symposium/crick.html.

31. Michael Michalko, *Thinkertoys: A Handbook of Creative Thinking Techniques,* Berkeley, CA: Ten Speed Press, 2006, and Dave Gray, *Gamestorming: A Playbook for Innovators, Rulebreakers, and Changemakers*, Sebastopol, CA: O'Reilly, 2010.

32. *Thinkpak: A Brainstorming Card Deck,* Berkeley, CA: Ten Speed Press, 2006.

33. Gray, *Gamestorming*, Kindle location 1795.

34. Chuck Frey, "The 7 All-time Greatest Ideation Techniques," *InnovationManagement.se*, May 30, 2013, http://www.innovationmanagement.se /2013/05/30/the-7-all-time-greatest-ideation-techniques/. See also a similar method here, "Reverse It," *Design Games, UX Mastery*, accessed December 6, 2016, http://www.designgames.com.au/reverse_it/.

35. Jared Spool's event, User Interface, held in the Boston area each year, https://www.uie.com/events/.

36. Bryan W. Mattimore, *Idea Stormers: How to Lead and Inspire Creative Breakthroughs* (San Francisco: Jossey-Bass, 2012).

37. See *Thinkertoys*, Kindle location 2258. See also some photos of our Lotus Blossom charts here: https://www.flickr.com/photos/nic221/sets/ 72157624129345469/with/4688629125/.

38. Diana Lillicrap, "The Lotus Blossom Technique," *5 by 5 Design*, August 18, 2011, http://5by5design.com/blog/design-practice/lotus-blossom-technique/, and "Lotus Blossom," *Creating Minds*, accessed December 6, 2016, http:// creatingminds.org/tools/lotus_blossom.htm.

39. *Thinkertoys,* Kindle Location 2270.

40. PSFK is a consulting firm. See their "Good Brands Reports" here: http:// www.psfk.com/tag/good-brands-report. Download a copy of the report we used here: http://hennigweb.com/keeping-up/good-brands-report.pdf.

CHAPTER 8

Moving Toward Implementation

Presenting to and Persuading Decision-Makers

After you've done some experimentation and testing of new technologies and service ideas, you'll need to do a good job of communicating with decision-makers on your staff about your ideas. In order to turn these ideas into fully supported services, you'll need the buy-in of people who set priorities and budgets in your organization.

When you've been immersed in learning and experimentation for quite some time, it's easy to forget that others may have never heard of these new technologies. If they have, they may only have heard a few tidbits, and not really have an understanding of what the technology can do or how it works. And quite often, they've read stories in the press about the dangers of these new technologies—so they may be feeling skeptical.

Beginner's Mind

What you'll need to do is change your mindset. Pretend that you know nothing about the technology in question. Start from the beginning and jot down notes that explain very clearly what the technology is and what it can do. Sometimes creating a "frequently asked questions" document can work as a first step. You may or may not use this formally, but it's a good way to make sure you can clearly explain things. You can also think through what some possible objections might be and address them.

These can serve as notes for yourself, to get you thinking in a way that will help you make a good presentation.

Emotions versus Logic

After reading several books about persuasion,[1] I realized that even though people ask for charts, logic, and statistics (because they feel themselves to be entirely rational in their decision-making), usually people are most persuaded by stories that appeal to their emotions. More than one expert refers to this.[2] So you'll need to be ready with both types of information.

According to Kerry Patterson, the author of *Influencer: the Power to Change Anything,*

> Poignant narratives help listeners transport themselves away from the content of what is being spoken and into the experience itself. Because they create vivid images and provide concrete detail, stories are more understandable than terse lectures. Because they focus on the simple reality of an actual event, stories are often more credible than simple statements of fact.[3]

It's great if during your experiments and your user needs studies, you've gathered both statistics and stories about your users. These will be valuable for creating persuasive presentations. For *quantitative* data, you can refer to results from your own library surveys, and also data from the world at large about users similar to yours. For example, Pew Research often has reports about library users that you can use to help make your case.[4]

For *qualitative* data, you can collect stories from user interviews, anonymous quotes from users who kept journals for your study, photographs of spaces (it's good to take photos where people aren't identifiable so you won't have to get permission to use them), video or audio recordings of particular problems that you've identified (that your proposed service will address), and summaries you've written based on stories from a few similar users.

Here's an example of how you might share your qualitative data with your staff in a way that's easy for them to remember. In 2010–2011 when we conducted our digital scholarship study at the MIT Libraries, one way that we made results easy to understand was by focusing on four specific themes, which are as follow:[5]

- Convenience wins
- Fragmentation hurts
- People count
- Place matters

For each of these themes, we made colorful printed cards (4 × 6 inches), that we handed out to everyone at our all-staff meetings where we presented our results.[6] The front of each card had the theme with an icon representing it. The reverse side had a quick summary, and quotes by students that we interviewed as examples. Our idea was that if our staff had something tangible to bring back to their offices, they could more easily remember the themes and use them when planning new service offerings. At a meeting with our whole staff where we presented the results of our study, our UX team members took turns telling the stories of individual students—stories we had learned about from our interviews.[7] These stories had our staff nodding and empathizing and led to some interesting ideas for improvements to our services.

Gathering themes like this is a standard part of qualitative data gathering,[8] and using the themes to group our stories was useful.

Tying Your Message to the Mission and Goals of Your Organization

In the section on criteria for evaluating your experiments, I included some examples of strategic goals of libraries, both academic and public. If you haven't already done this, now is a good time to find those documents from your own organization. Read through them and think about how your proposed idea will help meet those goals. Including this in your presentations can be very effective, because often the people who devised those goals are the same people who make decisions about money and staff time. They have proposed that your organization achieve certain goals and you are proposing a concrete way to do that.

Presentation Formats: Written Reports

Depending on your situation, when it comes time to propose your project, you may be asked to write a report, do a live presentation, or just sit down and talk informally in a meeting (or some combination of these). No matter what the format, it pays to learn how to communicate well in these types of situations.

If you are writing a grant proposal, that is a different story, with its own set of guidelines that you must follow. But with this type of work, usually you are proposing projects to managers in your own institution—projects that they will allocate time or budgets to, *if* they agree that it's a priority.

If you've been asked to create a written report, it helps to use the best practices for "writing for the web"—concise guidelines that usability

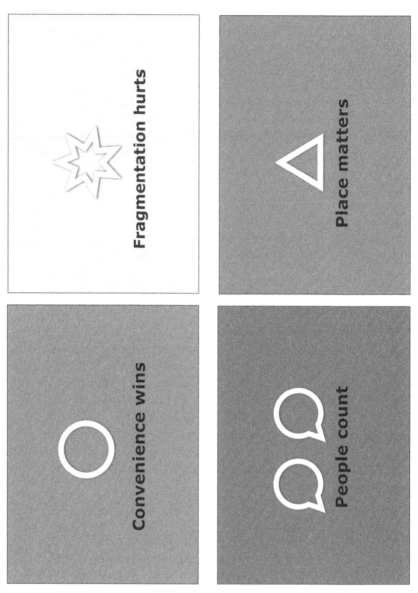

Figure 8.1: UX theme cards, front side, MIT Libraries Digital Scholarship Study, 2011

experts have shown to be effective on websites.[9] These guidelines emphasize being concise, using headings, bulleted lists, breaking up long paragraphs with useful images, and many more tips that will help make your document easy to scan and understand quickly. The last thing you want is a long, boring document that follows the style of academic writing. You might even consider making a slide deck (we'll discuss how to make effective slides later), and saving it as a PDF that can be distributed

MIT Libraries User Experience Group

Convenience wins

Convenience is highly prized, beyond technology, scholarship, or comprehensiveness. Users rely on familiar sources, technologies, and features, which can lead to a lack of knowledge about what might be more efficient, relevant, or authentic.

"I know that a library search would give more legitimate results, but Google is just so easy."
- Mechanical engineering grad student

"I could have [used MATLAB] on the MIT server, but I don't know how it functions. I've never used it. ... I don't know anything about the MIT server." Since she had already invested time in Chicago's system, she wanted to keep using that.
- Economics grad student

"When I'm on campus and need a book from a library, I almost always look up on-the-go on my phone which library the book is at." She uses iPhone apps for notes, email and Wikipedia, which she referred to as her "external hard drive."
- TA for an anthropology class

"I learned that [citation software] exists, but I never use it. When I do a bibliography, I just do it by hand, I don't know the advantage of that software."
- Economics grad student

MIT Libraries User Experience Group

People count

Collaboration means more than we expected. It means group work, but can also mean working individually toward a single shared product, working with people outside your discipline, or just working together on separate things.

"I think I would gain from group work, but no one is doing the same research in my field."
- Mechanical engineering grad student

Expertise is sought when asking for help, but familiarity or a referral often defines who gets asked for help.

"I usually ask my husband for help when I have technical questions (he's a course 6 grad)."
- Mechanical engineering grad student

"There is usually no one to ask (for specialized research). When it's something a bit more general, I ask my office mate."
- Economics grad student

MIT Libraries User Experience Group

Fragmentation hurts

Information overload + multiple storage solutions = fragmentation.

"I have an office here and at home and I travel often. I have these file folders (paper) and I go by topic. I put notes for each topic in folders. If I go somewhere, I pull the folders for the topics I'll work on, on those days."
- Economics grad student

"I struggle with printing & storing papers. To carry them with me, perhaps an iPad or Kindle would help with this?"
- Mechanical engineering grad student

A group used a wiki for their class notes, photos & videos, but they didn't know how to add videos to it. "The wiki is bad for that, and no one knows how to do that. We have some videos, and those we are just sitting on people's computers."
- Mechanical engineering undergrad

"It would be really awesome to work [in the library] late at night." She explained that at a certain point in the group's project, they needed technical information. "It would have been ... helpful at 1 or 2 AM to go to the library that had information on agricultural stuff."
- undergrad in Terrascope

MIT Libraries User Experience Group

Place matters

People appreciate the unique features of the places they choose to work.

"... I also went to the Barker Library... The atmosphere under the dome helps me be more productive."
- Mechanical engineering grad student

"I enjoy libraries with a lot of natural light: Hayden & Rotch."
- Task survey comment from an undergrad

"I prefer working here (Dewey) to my campus office. Better facilities, quieter, access to materials."
- Task survey comment from a grad student

A user's physical & emotional needs contribute to the place they choose to work.

This user talked about preferring her apartment to the library: "I have everything I need right there, all my books." She keeps "academic books, poetry, travel guides, all side by side. It makes the scholarly books seem down to earth."
- HASTS grad student/TA

This user studies in the Green building lounge. "They have cookie time every day at 3:00, the coffee machine gives you free coffee & hot cocoa, it's nice & bright, with comfy couches, and there are not too many people there."
- Undergrad in geology class

Figure 8.2: UX theme cards, reverse side, MIT Libraries Digital Scholarship Study, 2011

as a document for people to read. Use the principles of storytelling discussed in the next section about giving a talk with slides.

Presentation Formats: A Talk with Slides

If you can do a presentation with slides, it's a good idea to learn from the experts on how to make your presentation persuasive. The most helpful expert that I've learned from is Nancy Duarte, who wrote *Slide:ology: The Art and Science of Creating Great Presentations* (O'Reilly, 2008), *Resonate: Present Visual Stories That Transform Audiences* (Wiley, 2010), and *Illuminate: Ignite Change Through Speeches, Stories, Ceremonies, and Symbols* (Portfolio/Penguin, 2016).[10] If you ever have a chance to attend one of her presentations in person, it's well worth your time. Reading any one of her books will also be time well spent. To get started, I recommend watching an 18-minute video of one of her presentations at TEDx East, available at: https://vimeo.com/20618288.

Duarte focuses on communicating ideas in a way that resonates, and she talks about ideas changing the world. She mentions that ideas are conveyed most effectively through stories. Stories have been used throughout history, and people react physically and emotionally to stories. Stories have heroes, and it's important to realize that you as the presenter are not the hero, your audience is. The basic structure of a story is this: there is a likable hero, then there is a roadblock that the hero has encountered, and finally, there is a situation where the hero emerges transformed. In her talk in the video mentioned above, she shows what effective story structure is, and maps that structure to two well-known talks, one by Steve Jobs when he first introduced the iPhone, and Martin Luther King's "I Have a Dream" speech. She then talks about her own life story, the obstacles she overcame, and encourages the audience to change the world (or their own sphere) in spite of obstacles.

Even if you think your work is only a very small part of your workplace or institution, you can take inspiration from her advice about changing the world. When you find ways to effectively use new technologies to help library users, you are changing the world. I find inspiration from her quote at the end of her talk in the video: "The future isn't a place that we're going to go. It's a place that *you* get to create."—Nancy Duarte.[11]

Presentation Formats: Informal Meetings

Even if you aren't asked to write a report or give a presentation, you can still use some of these principles in small, informal meetings. Let's say you have 15–20 minutes to discuss your idea with your supervisor or with a small group. Be prepared with a story. Use the story arc recommended by Nancy Duarte. Your library user is the hero, the obstacle is the user need you've identified, and the transformation is how your users' lives will be improved by using your new service. Bring a few statistics, know some real-life stories from your experiments, and perhaps bring a one-page handout that answers questions about your proposed service. Remember to tie it in with your library's strategic goals. Make your handout very brief, with bulleted lists. Focus on how your users' lives will be improved, rather than the technical details of the new technology.

Sometimes, you'll need to get permission just to run an experiment. You can use this same method to get permission for that. Emphasize that it's just an experiment, show how you will frame it that way to users, and emphasize that your staff doesn't need to be trained on how to support something new for this experiment. Show them your criteria for evaluating success and your plan for "graveyarding" or "graduating" each experiment at regular intervals, as discussed in the previous chapter. Managers are often faced with situations where resources are spread too thin, and it's usually good news to them when you discuss ruling out some of your experiments.

Keep in mind that while you might be enthusiastic about the potential of a new technology (because you've been immersing yourself in knowledge about it and seeing how it can help users), others in your organization have been busy focusing on running a complex institution and have many other things on their minds. So be brief and be prepared, by using these techniques.

Dealing with Naysayers

It seems that every workgroup has someone (or more than one person) who is known for shooting down ideas that involve new technologies. Instead of getting discouraged by this, learn to expect it and use it as an opportunity. Knowing that your ideas are likely to get shot down is good motivation for being very well prepared.

If you have a chance to tell your story in a group setting and you use the ideas above, that's great. You're in a strong place. Try to get permission to present your whole story (concisely), before taking questions and discussion. If you can do that, it's likely that people other than the naysayer will help defend your idea.

Usually, it helps if the negative people feel heard and that their objections are being taken seriously. Be sure to listen carefully and reflect back what their concerns are. Then use your stories and statistics to respond to their concerns. Write down their objections and show that you have or will make a plan for dealing with them. If you are a person who is enthusiastic about experimenting with new technologies, you might not have a good understanding of the difficulties faced by others in your organization who need to support technology. So it's good to show that you are taking their concerns seriously and will follow through with ways to address them.

If you are dealing with an especially difficult person who has more power than you do in your organization, it can help to find allies who are their peers and approach them in advance. If you can make these alliances, often those allies will be willing to listen to your proposals, and will help you convince their peers.

This is a situation that you probably understand if you've worked in any organization for very long. Remember that in the world of experimenting with new technologies, it's even more likely that you'll need to prepare for this, since there is a long tradition of people fearing new technologies.[12]

As an information professional, you are in a good position to find the balance between unrealistic optimism, and a dystopian pessimism that often stops discussions of implementing new technologies. I like to use the term, "rational optimist," which is also the title of a book by Matt Ridley.[13] If you would like to think about the issue of technology optimism versus technology pessimism in more depth, you may enjoy an article by Jay Ogilvy, "Facing the Fold: From the Eclipse of Utopia to the Restoration of Hope."[14] In it, he makes the case for a position he calls "a scenaric stance." This is a viewpoint that holds both optimistic and pessimistic scenarios in your mind at the same time. He says, "One is relieved of the naiveté of callow optimism, even as one is spared the amoral defeatism of the all-knowing cynic. You've looked at the dark side; you've seen the very real risk; and still you're able to move ahead constructively. . ..having made a choice in full knowledge of the alternatives and the risks involved, you'll act deliberately and resolutely, but not rashly or foolishly."

Getting Approved: Next Steps

Once your project is approved, you're ready to move to the next step—implementation. In the next section, we'll discuss why it's a good idea to use different people on your staff to implement new services and not the emerging technologies librarian.

Passing on Projects to Implementers

In the beginning of this book, I talked about the idea of two types of people, visionaries and implementers. You may find yourself somewhere between these two types—it's a continuum. It's likely though that you will find yourself leaning more in one of these directions than the other. Of course, we need both sets of skills and talents in any organization. I've addressed both types of people in this book and I hope you can see yourself and your colleagues in this discussion and benefit from the methods and tips that I've found so useful.

As a reminder, following is the list of qualities that I've grouped as either "visionary" or "implementer." It's probably no surprise to you that I personally lean toward the role of visionary.

The Visionary

- has the ability to look at the big picture without getting bogged down in details.
- does not easily get overwhelmed when faced with a deluge of information.
- is good at thinking creatively and combining ideas from different fields.
- has a desire to be an "early adopter" (taking it in stride if things break).
- has a strong curiosity about emerging technologies and where they might lead.
- has a sense of optimism about the possibilities of new technologies.
- is a continual learner, with a love for learning.
- is good at communicating in interesting ways that grab your emotions as well as your intellect.

The Implementer

- is good at working with and understanding specific details.
- is good at evaluating and organizing information.
- is good at understanding the results of user needs studies.
- prefers to use new technologies after others have tested them and they are more mature and more solid.
- is good at thinking linearly and understanding cause and effect.
- has a healthy skepticism about new technologies and possible pitfalls.
- asks interesting questions about each new technology.
- is good at project management, leading teams, and making sure details get carried out correctly.

Splitting the Work

Now that it's time to implement a new service, you want to rely on the skill set of expert implementers. This is a good time for those involved in the experiments, evaluations, and persuading others that a project should happen, to hand off their work to people with this complementary skill set.

Too often, I've seen situations where the same people were asked to do all of this work. Instead, it's better if you allow the visionaries to go back to exploring other new technologies. And let the implementers do what they are good at—project management and the details of setting up a new service.

Sometimes people, who are good with technology in any way at all, get lumped together into one group in the minds of those writing the job descriptions. But someone who is really good at handling tech support for your users, for example, may fall into either role, depending on their talents and dispositions. So I recommend viewing your staff through this lens as a way to help decide who works on what and as a way to write job descriptions.

Of course, you will want to have some overlap when a new project is getting off the ground. You'll need someone who was part of the early exploration to be involved. Sometimes they can train other staff members and then move off the project or become an advisor to it. Other times someone who is in the middle of the continuum of skill sets is a good person to be on the team and could do a bit of both roles.

If you are in a very small organization, it's likely that you have to learn many skills and do everything, and you're used to that. But you can still benefit from this way of viewing people and try to assign the visionary work and implementation to those most suited to it. You may work with outside consultants from time to time, or partner with people outside of your library (such as faculty members, teachers, or others in your organization but outside of the library). If possible, aim for complementary skill sets to work together, rather than having one person or team do everything.

Job Descriptions

In the next chapter, I'll discuss how to write job descriptions for an "emerging technologies librarian" or similar role. We'll look at some sample job descriptions and talk about what to do if you are part of a large organization, a small one, or are working as a one-person librarian.

Endnotes

1. Such as Noah J. Goldstein, Steve J. Martin, and Robert B. Cialdini, *Yes!: 50 Scientifically Proven Ways to Be Persuasive*, New York: Free Press, 2010, Robert Sutton, *Weird Ideas That Work, New York: Free Press, 2007,* and Robert B. Cialdini, *Influence: The Psychology of Persuasion,* New York: Collins, 2007.

2. See Patterson, Kerry. *Influencer: The Power to Change Anything,* New York: McGraw-Hill, 2008, Kindle location 1072.

3. Ibid, Kindle location 1253.

4. Pew Research Center: Internet, Science and Tech, http://www.pewinternet .org/. See their Presentations page for useful summaries of recent data and statistics about libraries, http://www.pewinternet.org/category/presentations/.

5. Learn more about this study in my presentation, "Academic E-Reading: Themes from User Experience Studies," November 8, 2011,http://www.slide share.net/nic221/academic-ereading-themes-from-user-experience-studies

6. Download a PDF copy of the cards here: http://hennigweb.com/keeping-up/ ux-theme-cards.pdf

7. We didn't reveal their names, of course—just whether they were a graduate or undergraduate student and which department they were from.

8. Gery W. Ryan and H. Russell Bernard, "Techniques to Identify Themes in Qualitative Data," Analytic Technologies, accessed December 6, 2016, http:// www.analytictech.com/mb870/readings/ryan- bernard_techniques_to_identify_themes_in.htm.

9. See this book by Janice (Ginny) Redish, *Letting Go of the Words, Second Edition: Writing Web Content that Works,* Waltham, MA: Morgan Kaufmann, 2014.

10. See also the author's website, http://www.duarte.com/perspective/#books.

11. "Nancy Duarte's Talk at TEDx East," https://vimeo.com/20618288 (at 17:55 in the video).

12. Vaughan Bell, "Don't Touch That Dial!," A history of media technology scares, from the printing press to Facebook, *Slate*, February 15, 2010, http:// www.slate.com/articles/health_and_science/science/2010/02/dont_touch_that _dial.single.html.

13. Matt Ridley, *The Rational Optimist: How Prosperity Evolves,* New York: Harper, 2010. This title inspired me when coming up with the name of a keynote talk I gave, "Librarians as Rational Optimists: Using Top Tech Trends to Build Our Future," eResource & Emerging Technologies Summit, Mississippi State University Libraries, August 4, 2012, http://hennigweb.com/presentations/ msuleets/hennig-rational-optimist.pdf.

14. Jay Ogilvy, "Facing the Fold From the Eclipse of Utopia to the Restoration of Hope," *Foresight*, 13(4), 7–23, http://www.emeraldinsight.com/doi/abs/ 10.1108/14636681111153931?journalCode=fs.

CHAPTER 9

Emerging Technologies Librarians— Defining Job Roles

In the beginning of this book, I discussed some of the challenges that libraries face with technology staffing. We looked at these factors:

- There is a growing need for technology-focused jobs in libraries.
- Many job postings emphasize trend-spotting and knowledge of emerging technology trends.
- There is a trend toward hiring "emerging technologies librarians," or including that role as a significant part of another job description.

But as the study by Radniecki[1] showed, the job descriptions are all over the map, and the role of "emerging technologies librarian" is often not clearly defined. Let's look into this issue a bit more in depth in this chapter.

Current Job Descriptions

It's interesting to take a look at current job descriptions for "emerging technologies librarian." I found some examples by searching Google for "emerging technologies librarian job description."

Let's look at a few of them. Before we do, I'd like to emphasize that I don't mean to criticize any job description, or the people who wrote them. I know very well the constraints that most libraries and library managers are working under, with tight budgets and not being able to increase their staff head count easily. We librarians are dedicated to bringing new technologies into our services and focusing on the needs of our users. And we're very creative with combining roles in order to get the necessary work done.

I'd like to look at these because it helps to examine real-world examples in order to think about different ways to combine this kind of work with other positions.

The following are excerpts from full descriptions. Here I'm focusing on the duties and also looking at what kinds of positions these are combined with. I'm not including the qualifications, since those vary greatly depending on what job they are combined with.

All emphasis below is mine (for easier skimming).

1. Emerging Technologies Librarian
University of Georgia Libraries

> The University of Georgia Libraries seeks a service-oriented and forward-thinking Emerging Technologies Librarian. The Emerging Technologies Librarian will be responsible to the Head of the Research & Instruction Department for assisting users in making effective use of information resources and *taking a leadership role in leveraging new technologies to meet the needs of scientific researchers.* To achieve these goals, the Emerging Technologies Librarian provides *in-person and virtual reference assistance, library instruction sessions, and one-on-one in-depth consultations* in all areas of the sciences. The Librarian also provides outreach and instruction for the Science Library MakerSpace and manages the Science Library website and social media presence.[2]

In this description, the job is combined with a reference and instruction librarian. They are also asked to manage the library Makerspace, the website, and their social media presence.

2. Librarian II—Emerging Technologies Librarian
West Linn Public Library, Oregon

> The City of West Linn is seeking an energetic Librarian II with a focus on Technology Leadership. Under the direction of the Library Director, this

position will assist in helping to **identify and promote** the use of emerging and existing technologies, and **collaborate with other librarians to provide innovative library services** designed to enrich the public library experience. This position will take **an active role in defining, planning, and implementing new technology and library related services for the West Linn Public Library and its patrons.** This position will serve as a **consultant and advisor** for library web development, web 2.0 and 3.0 technologies, social networking, software training for the public, gaming, podcasting, video, e-learning services, maker space innovations, and other current and future technologies. This position will help the West Linn Library with current technology trends, and of emerging and evolving ideas and technological tools for library and information management via research, professional literature, online resources, professional development activities, and personal networking

This position will **provide leadership in library services** related to technological applications including multimedia technologies, and **teach library staff members how to use and integrate emerging technologies** into public services, with social media creation and implementation.
This position will also have **reference, collection development,** and task force committee and library duties as assigned.[3]

In this public library position, the job is focused on identifying and promoting emerging technologies as well as collaborating with other librarians on the implementation of services. They are also asked to serve as consultant and advisor on various services and programs related to new technologies, as well as teach other library staff members about new technologies. It's combined with a reference librarian position.

3. Emerging Technologies Librarian
University of Notre Dame

The individual in this position will be responsible for **assisting users with the identification, evaluation, and use of emerging technologies in the creation of a variety of media-rich projects.** S/he will **explore, develop, promote, and assess innovative online tools** and related services for library learners and identify learning and engagement opportunities to support student research and promote student success.

A significant task will be to **maintain and expand a website (https:// remix.nd.edu/) that promotes and supports student creation of media-rich projects.**S/he will **help students individually and in the classroom setting to identify and use a variety of digital media** in their assignments, and s/he will work collaboratively with teaching faculty, especially those in the

Multimedia Writing & Rhetoric program, to identify ways to incorporate media-rich assignments into student coursework.

This person will help to **identify, monitor, assess, and relay information about new and emerging technologies of interest to the Library,** including recommendations for adoption. S/he will work collaboratively with a dynamic group of library colleagues to provide point of need reference services, course-integrated library instruction, library workshops, and a variety of outreach activities. S/he will also work with librarians to **create and implement online learning modules to support both information and digital literacy.**[4]

In this description, the job is combined with an instruction-focused position for a specific program. They are asked to work with colleagues on reference, instruction, and workshops and to create online learning modules, as well as to maintain a special website for student creation of media-rich projects.

4. User Experience and Emerging Technologies Librarian

Columbia College Chicago

> The User Experience and Emerging Technologies Librarian **identifies, implements, and evaluates current and emerging technologies** for the delivery of library services, with a special **focus on reference and instructional** services, including virtual reference, discovery tools, social networking applications, mobile services, and instructional technologies; **plans, develops and evaluates the Columbia College Chicago Library website;** and ensures that Library services and instructional products are easy and pleasurable to use. This librarian **tracks trends, assesses user needs and preferences, investigates new developments and applications, and incorporates appropriate technologies into the Library environment.**
>
> The User Experience and Emerging Technologies Librarian **collaborates to plan staff development opportunities** for building technology awareness and supports Library staff in using and adopting technologies that improve user experience.
>
> The User Experience and Emerging Technologies Librarian's duties include:
>
> - **Planning, developing and evaluating the Columbia College Chicago Library website** and serving as liaison between the Library and campus IT for Library website content management.

- **Building staff awareness** of new and emerging technologies Encouraging the adoption of technologies that improve the Library's physical and virtual presence.

- **Creating widgets, apps and other products** that embed resources and services into learning management systems such as Moodle.

- **Assessing the impact of technology-based services on Library users.**

- **Collecting and reporting usage statistics** and other user input and data.

- **Advising and assisting in efforts to use emerging technologies to build relationships with users** and increase awareness of Library resources and services in the campus community.[5]

In this description, the job is combined with a user experience librarian, so it has a big focus on assessing user needs. It also includes managing their website and planning staff development.

5. Systems/Emerging Technologies Librarian
Biddle Law Library, University of Pennsylvania Law School

> The Systems/Emerging Technologies Librarian plays a unique role in **ensuring that the Biddle Law Library takes full advantage of existing technologies as well as investigates and adopts new technologies** in acquiring, organizing, and presenting legal information to its faculty, students, and other users outside the law school. Bridging both the traditional technical services and public services departments, the librarian **provides key support for the library's integrated library system, works with all the librarians and other members of the law school to create content for the library website,** and plays a key role in i**dentifying new technologies** for the library to incorporate into its teaching and research activities.

The Systems/Emerging Technologies Librarian performs the following duties:

- Responsible for the overall **administration**, customization, maintenance and troubleshooting of the library's **integrated library system**, currently Innovative Interfaces, Inc. Millennium (soon to be Sierra), including the WebPAC and the Encore discovery tool;

- Monitors system performance; suggests and coordinates system software and hardware upgrades; monitors system security; trains staff on system modules and new releases, writes relevant documentation;

monitors industry developments and recommends adoption of new programs when appropriate;

- Serves as liaison to library staff, patrons, and the ILS vendor regarding system issues;

- With other librarians, evaluates, **designs, and creates a variety of web resources and applications** that promote research and instructional activities;

- **Identifies, evaluates, implements, and maintains new and emerging library-related technologies** and applications that will benefit both patrons and library staff;

- Works with the Electronic Resources and Serials Librarian to **implement, maintain, and troubleshoot access to electronic resources,** systems integration with other campus resources, other systems-related projects;

- **Assists the Associate Director of Technical Services with statistics and reporting,** especially related to budget, expenditures, and materials counts;

- In conjunction with the Archivist, **undertakes and leads digitization projects when** appropriate;

- Collaborates with other members of the library and law school staff to **identify user needs.**[6]

In this description, the job is combined with the role of a systems librarian who is managing the ILS. The system librarian works with the e-resources librarian to maintain and troubleshoot access to e-resources, sometimes lead digitization projects, and work on identifying user needs.

These are just a few examples. It's interesting to look at what kinds of positions an "emerging technologies librarian" is combined with, and what kinds of skills are asked for. In the previously mentioned article by Radniecki, she talks about job descriptions being "varied and vague." I wouldn't say that these descriptions are vague, but they certainly are varied. They often combine many kinds of work into one position. I understand the necessity for that, given most library budgets and staffing constraints, and I have some ideas for defining this type of role effectively.

If you are faced with writing a new description and want to include the role of "emerging technologies librarian," I have some ideas for how to use the concepts in this book to craft your positions and write descriptions that take advantage of the best talents that different librarians have. Let's look at that in the next section.

Defining This Type of Position for Your Organization

So how might you use the concepts I've described in this book—the so-called visionaries vs. implementers? If you are fortunate enough to have the budget for it, you might want to create an entire position called "Emerging Technologies Librarian." Or you might want to combine these skills with other positions in your library. Either way, I'd like to suggest using the continuum that I mentioned in the beginning.

Following again is the list of qualities.

The Visionary

- has the ability to look at the big picture without getting bogged down in details.
- does not easily get overwhelmed when faced with a deluge of information.
- is good at thinking creatively and combining ideas from different fields.
- has a desire to be an "early adopter" (taking it in stride if things break).
- has a strong curiosity about emerging technologies and where they might lead.
- has a sense of optimism about the possibilities of new technologies.
- is a continual learner, with a love for learning.
- is good at communicating in interesting ways that grab your emotions as well as your intellect.

The Implementer

- is good at working with and understanding specific details.
- is good at evaluating and organizing information.
- is good at understanding the results of user needs studies.
- prefers to use new technologies after others have tested them and they are more mature and more solid.
- is good at thinking linearly and understanding cause and effect.
- has a healthy skepticism about new technologies and possible pitfalls.
- asks interesting questions about each new technology.
- is good at project management, leading teams, and making sure details get carried out correctly.

There is more than one way that you could approach this. Let's start with creating an entire position called "emerging technologies librarian." An emerging technologies librarian should be focused on the visionary side of the continuum.

One Role: Emerging Technologies Librarian

If you are aiming for this solution, I would define this role as primarily a visionary role. Use the qualities and talents from the visionary list to define the position.

The goal for this librarian would be to focus on scanning the horizon, continually researching and evaluating new technologies. They would combine new technology ideas with an understanding of users in order to define experiments, evaluate them, and propose them as services to decision-makers. They might advise on implementation projects and train other staff (implementers) on new technologies, but their focus would be mostly on continual exploration and evaluation—not on implementation.

This doesn't mean they might not also need and use some skills from the implementer list, but primarily they would work as a visionary.

Combined Role—Emerging Technologies as Part of Another Job

If you need to combine this role with another position, think about what kind of position goes well with the visionary role. In a medium-to-large organization, often this will be someone at a manager level or higher. This kind of vision work goes well with roles who are involved with strategic planning. It could go together with someone managing your IT staff, or head of your user experience group.

Alternatively, and perhaps more likely in a smaller library, this role could be combined with any general librarian role, such as a subject specialist or instruction librarian in an academic library, a youth services librarian in a public library, or an information researcher in a corporate library. Some-one who works directly with your users and has the kind of talents in the visionary list would be well suited.

Two Roles: Emerging Technologies Visionary and Emerging Technologies Implementer

Another way to break this up would be to create two kinds of emerging technologies librarians, one as a visionary and one as implementer. They could work together in a team or department to lead the entire process as described in this book, with some overlap, but mostly focusing on their own skill set.

If you can't afford to have two entire positions like this, you could use the combined role idea above to define these as half of two different positions. For the implementer role, think about which other positions in your organization use detailed implementation skills—it could be someone who is an IT support person, an ILS manager, an application developer, a cataloger, archivist, or anyone who is very good at this detailed kind of implementation work and has an interest in new technologies. For the visionary role, consider positions where visioning, future planning, and understanding user needs is part of the role, such as a user experience librarian, an instruction or reference librarian, a manager who plans for the future of IT in your organization, or similar roles.

Sometimes it's not about the actual position, but more about the talent you have in various people on your staff. Visionaries and implementers might be found in any position.

Defining the Duties

You have the lists above to use for defining the qualities, talents, and dispositions of people for this role. Now let's define some duties that you might want to include in your job descriptions.

These duties are in order beginning with the visionary role, continuing through toward an implementer role.

Vision and exploration

- Continuously scan the literature in all media formats in order to keep up with technology trends.
- Attend relevant conferences, online training, and local meet-ups.
- Network with colleagues in diverse technology fields.
- Follow ethical debates around new technologies.
- Promote and advocate for diversity and inclusion related to new technologies.
- Promote and advocate for accessibility of new technologies.

Beginning to evaluate

- Take useful notes, and document your learning for your own use.
- Curate information for colleagues in your library and other libraries.

- Spot trends and learn to distinguish them from fads.
- Lead projects using the design thinking process.

Ideation and innovation

- Implement ideation practices for coming up with innovative ideas.
- Create opportunities for hands-on play with new technologies for your colleagues and your users.

Heading toward implementation

- Design small experiments for promising new technologies.
- Develop criteria for evaluating those experiments and use critical thinking skills when evaluating.
- Present and persuade decision-makers when you have a proposal for a service using new technologies.
- Pass on projects to implementers when a new service is approved.

Of course, you will want to customize these for your particular position. The main point is to keep the concept of visionary versus implementer in mind as two complementary skill sets.

Defining Qualifications

The qualifications will depend entirely on which type of job you are describing. If you're combining this with another role, you'll have specific qualifications for that role. For the emerging technologies part of the description, I'd like to suggest that you use the list of qualities above as a starting point. Select appropriate skills and talents depending on whether this is mostly a visionary or implementer position. Of course, my lists are mostly "soft skills." You'll also likely need to define some "hard skills," such as particular experience with tools, technologies, and best practices for the specific job.

As I mentioned in the beginning of this book, there are some skills that every library wants in its entire staff, such as the following:

- A strong sense of empathy for users
- Knowing how to work well with diverse groups of people
- A love of continuous learning
- Being good at teamwork and collaboration
- Being an effective communicator

You will of course include skills like those.

Following are some specific "hard skills" that you might want to include in the qualifications as well.

- Knowledge of design thinking methodology
- Familiarity with established user experience practices, especially qualitative research methods
- Familiarity with diversity standards for your institution or the library profession
- Familiarity with accessibility standards related to web and mobile design (or newer technologies)
- Familiarity with best practices for creating concise and useful presentations about new technologies
- Experience with creating effective instruction for new technologies, both in-person and online

You'll notice that I said "familiarity with," rather than "deep knowledge of" for some of those items. That's because you don't need to expect a person to have deep knowledge of user experience research unless they've been trained or had experience in that field (unless you are combining this with a user experience position—which can be a good combination). Instead, they only need to be able to list a few qualitative research methods and what kinds of results you can expect to learn from them. The same applies to the other knowledge-based qualifications—they should have basic familiarity, no need to be an expert in all of them.

What to Do If You Are a Very Small Organization

If you are from a very small library with only one to three staff members, you might be wondering how to best include this kind of work. In the past, I've worked in a 1-person music library (Longy School of Music in Cambridge, Massachusetts), a 2-person special library (the Electronic Frontier Foundation), a 4-person corporate library (Bose Corporation), a small college library with about 8 staff members (Emmanuel College in Boston), and a medium-sized academic library with about 200 staff members (The MIT Libraries). So, I'm familiar with needing to be a "jack-of-all trades" librarian.

As a start, I would suggest thinking about where you and your staff fit on the visionaries-to-implementers continuum and following the advice in "Visionaries and Implementers—Strategies for Each" section of Chapter 3.

If you or one of your staff identifies more as a visionary, assign this type of work as part of the role. If you don't have the time or resources to do a user needs study, you can use information from studies done by those who have studied users similar to your own. You can also find good advice in a book by Leah Buley called *The User Experience Team of One: A Research and Design Survival Guide.*[7]

If your entire staff mainly fits on the implementer side of the continuum, look for chances to work with outside consultants who are on the visionary side. They may be able to work on short-term projects to do the kind of work that visionaries do, including recommending a new service and training your staff. You may also be able to collaborate with others in your institution if you are a small library inside of a larger organization. Make alliances with others who can work with you on projects that benefit all.

And finally, you can aim to hire someone with complementary qualities to your staff next time you have an open position that would combine well with this type of work. Use my list of qualities for visionaries to bring people with those talents and dispositions into your organization.

Diversity and "Performance-Based Job Descriptions"

I'd like to encourage the practice of "performance-based hiring," which is a method that focuses on being able to achieve comparable results with experiences from types of organizations other than your own. Not only does this bring fresh ideas into your organization but it's a method that can help you achieve a more diverse workforce. The ACRL's Diversity Standards include a focus on workplace diversity that emphasizes the support of diversity in recruitment, hiring, and retention.[8]

Studies have shown that having a diverse workforce leads to more innovation. In a 2013 article from Harvard Business Review, the following point was made:

> ... diversity unlocks innovation by creating an environment where "outside the box" ideas are heard. When minorities form a critical mass and leaders value differences, all employees can find senior people to go to bat for compelling ideas and can persuade those in charge of budgets to deploy resources to develop those ideas.[9]

So what is a "performance-based job description?" According to Lou Adler, the author of *Hire with Your Head: Using Performance-Based Hiring to Build Great Teams*,[10] this type of description "describes the work that a person needs to successfully accomplish during the first year on the job."[11] It focuses on the specifics of what the person is being asked to achieve, rather than exact experience that the applicant needs to have (such as a certain number of years of experience). This is a good way to approach job descriptions for several reasons. Often there are candidates who don't have long experience, but have the ability to learn quickly and the talent for that your specific type of work. There are also candidates with many years of experience, but in another field or context, who are quick learners and have the talent you need.

You can see how this approach helps to prevent age discrimination (for both young and old). It can also help you be inclusive with other talented candidates who come from diverse backgrounds of different kinds, including people who haven't worked recently because of military service, parenting duties, or recovering from accidents and injuries.

Performance-Based Duties

So going back to my lists of duties above, it's time to get specific about what you want the person in this position to do during their first year. You could use phrases like the following:

- Explore emerging technologies in order to come up with three to five small technology experiments in your first year.

- Develop criteria for evaluating those experiments, based on user needs, diversity standards, accessibility standards, and our library's strategic goals.

- Recommend one to two new services using new technologies in your first year and work collaboratively as an advisor with others on our staff who will be implementing those services.

Define the other duties and skills in the same way, for the other work you are combining this with.

Template for Your Job Description

Here's a template and structure that you might find useful when developing your job description.

Sample Structure

- Name of organization and the position title

- Closing date

- Location

- Brief description

- What you'll do: (list)

- Is this a good fit for you? We're looking for a person who can: (list)

- Your experience and educational background (list of educational requirements, "knowledge of...." "Familiarity with...." etc.)

- Who are we?

- What's it like to work at ....?

- Our benefits

- How to apply

Fictional Job Description

Following is an idea for a job description for an emerging technologies librarian.

XZZ Library, Emerging Technologies Librarian

Closing date: 1/1/0000

Location: City, State, Country

Description

We're seeking an emerging technologies librarian for a full-time position. In this role, you'll explore new technologies in order to come up with three to five small technology experiments in your first year. You'll develop criteria for evaluating those experiments, based on user needs, diversity standards, accessibility standards, and our library's strategic goals. By the end of your first year, you will recommend one to two new services that use new technologies. You will also work as an advisor with others on our staff who will be implementing those services.

What You'll Do
Vision and exploration

- Scan the literature in all media formats in order to keep up with technology trends.

- Attend relevant conferences, online training, and local meet-ups.

- Network with colleagues in diverse technology fields.

- Follow ethical debates around new technologies.

- Promote and advocate for diversity and inclusion related to new technologies.

- Promote and advocate for accessibility of new technologies.

Evaluation

- Take useful notes, and document your learning for your own use.
- Curate information for colleagues in your library and other libraries.
- Spot trends and learn to distinguish from fads.
- Lead projects using the design thinking process.

Ideation and innovation

- Implement ideation practices for coming up with innovative ideas.
- Create opportunities for hands-on play with new technologies for your colleagues and your users.

Heading toward implementation

- Design small experiments for promising new technologies.
- Develop criteria for evaluating those experiments and use critical thinking skills when evaluating.
- Present and persuade decision-makers when you have a proposal for a service using new technologies.
- Pass on projects to implementers when a new service is approved.
- Train your colleagues on what they need to know about new technologies that are going to be implemented in library services.

Is This a Good Fit for You? We're Looking for a Person Who

- has the ability to look at the big picture without getting bogged down in details.
- does not easily get overwhelmed when faced with a deluge of information.
- is good at thinking creatively and combining ideas from different fields.
- has a desire to be an "early adopter" (taking it in stride if things break).
- has a strong curiosity about emerging technologies and where they might lead.
- has a sense of optimism about the possibilities of new technologies.
- is a continual learner, with a love of learning.
- can communicate effectively in interesting ways that grab your emotions as well as your intellect.

Your Experience and Educational Background

- A master's degree in library science

- Knowledge of design thinking methodology

- Familiarity with established user experience practices, especially qualitative research methods

- Familiarity with diversity standards for this institution and the library profession

- Familiarity with accessibility standards related to web and mobile design (or other new technologies)

- Familiarity with best practices for creating concise and useful presentations about new technologies

- Experience with creating effective instruction for new technologies, both in-person and online

Who Are We?
Describe your workplace and the mission of your institution.

What's It Like to Work at XYZ Library?
Talk about the advantages of working there, especially for professional growth.

Our Benefits
Describe your benefits package.

XYZ Library is an inclusive and accessible employer committed to employment equity objectives and invites applications from all qualified individuals.

To apply.... (Fill in your details).

Summary

As you can see, I recommend defining this position as a visionary role. It's great if you can make it a full-time position as described above. If not, try to combine it with a position where the visionary qualities make sense. When it comes to implementation, an emerging technologies librarian can advise, train, and collaborate with implementers in other roles on your staff, and then be free to continue the cycle of exploring new technologies again.

Focus your descriptions on specific measurable goals that you want them to achieve in their first year. Judge candidates on their ability to achieve those goals, rather than on their having had the exact same experience in an institution similar to yours.

Endnotes

1. Tara Radniecki, "Study on Emerging Technologies Librarians: How a New Library Position and Its Competencies Are Evolving to Meet the Technology and Information Needs of Libraries and Their Patrons," Paper presented at: IFLA WLIC 2013—Singapore—Future Libraries: Infinite Possibilities in Session 152 —Reference and Information Services, http://library.ifla.org/id/eprint/134.

2. Excerpt from job description, http://www.georgialibraries.org/jobs/index.php ?post_id=2428.

3. Excerpt from job description, https://westlinnoregon.gov/humanresources/ librarian-iiemerging-technologies-librarian.

4. Excerpt from job description, https://library.nd.edu/about/employment/ documents/EmergingTechnologiesLibrarianPD_rev_000.pdf

5. Excerpt from job description, https://www.carli.illinois.edu/user-experience -and-emerging-technologies-librarian-columbia-college-chicago.

6. Excerpt from job description, https://www.law.upenn.edu/live/files/1673 -systems-amp-emerging-technologies-librarian.

7. Leah Buley, *The User Experience Team of One: A Research and Design Survival Guide,* Brooklyn, NY: Rosenfeld Media, 2013.

8. "Diversity Standards: Cultural Competency for Academic Libraries (2012)," Association of College and Research Libraries, accessed December 6, 2016, http://www.ala.org/acrl/standards/diversity. See standard 7: Workforce Diversity.

9. Sylvia Ann Hewlett, Melinda Marshall, and Laura Sherbin, "How Diversity Can Drive Innovation," *Harvard Business Review,* December 2013, https:// hbr.org/2013/12/how-diversity-can-drive-innovation.

10. Lou Adler, *Hire with Your Head: Using Performance-Based Hiring to Build Great Teams, Hoboken,* NJ: John Wiley & Sons, 2007.

11. Adler, quoted in Dan Wisniewski, "Why you should ditch job descriptions . . . or maybe not," HR Morning, May 3, 2013, http://www.hrmorning.com/ ditch-job-descriptions-maybe/.

CHAPTER 10

Epilogue

I hope that by reading through the ideas in this book, you now feel a sense of optimism about your ability to keep up with emerging technologies. Whether you identify more with the qualities of a "visionary" or an "implementer" you now have some strategies for keeping up.

When you use methods like those described in this book, you can integrate new technologies into the design of library services that make a strong positive difference in the lives of your users. You can use established methods for everything from gathering information about technologies to gathering information about the needs of your users. You can evaluate this information by aligning it with user needs, the latest standards for diversity and accessibility, the values of your institution and of the library profession, and your institution's strategic goals.

In addition, you can design experiments that will help you decide which technologies to use in library services based on real-world feedback. You can learn to create effective presentations about new technologies that will help persuade the decision-makers who set priorities and budgets. And you can pass approved projects on to those in your organization with the strongest talents for implementation.

If you are responsible for hiring and writing job descriptions, you can use the suggestions here for separating "visionaries" and "implementers" into separate but overlapping roles. And you can write your job descriptions based on measurable goals (performance-based job descriptions), which helps you to hire more diverse staff, which, in turn, can lead to more innovative ideas within your organization.

Libraries have been experimenting with and implementing innovative services using new technologies, both in recent years and throughout history. For some inspiring recent examples, read about The Knight Foundation's Future of Libraries project, http://www.knightfoundation.org/topics/future-of-libraries. For an audio program about it, try this episode of a podcast called "Circulating Ideas," https://circulatingideas.com/2016/06/23/episode-95-knight-news-challenge-on-libraries-winners/, where Steve Thomas interviews John Bracken about the 2016 challenge winners.

I'm confident that libraries will continue to innovate, and I hope that having specific methods at hand in this book will make it easier for you to innovate in your library. I also hope that you will refer to this book as a handy compilation of best practices in years to come, no matter which technologies are on the horizon.

I welcome feedback on how this book has helped you, along with any ideas you have for additions or improvements. You can contact me at http://nicolehennig.com/contact-me/. Thanks for reading, and good luck with designing innovative library services using new technologies!

CHAPTER 11

Resource Guide

Bibliography: Books, Blogs, Articles, Websites

I've relied on many experts from outside the world of library and
information science and I hope that bringing those resources together
in this book will be helpful to you.

Be sure to scan all of the endnotes in each chapter. This bibliography
includes the most important of those along with additional resources for
continuing your learning. I've included books, blogs, articles, reports, and
websites. For multimedia sources, see the chapter near the beginning of
this book, "Multimedia resources: video, audio, and courses."

Skimming and Scanning

Cassidy, Vicki. "Beyond Bookmarks: The 10 Best Read It Later Apps for
Saving Articles and Videos." August 25, 2105, https://zapier.com/blog/
best-bookmaking-read-it-later-app/.

Marks Beale, Abby. "Skimming And Scanning: Two Important
Strategies For Speeding Up Your Reading." February 4, 2013, http://
www.howtolearn.com/2013/02/skimming-and-scanning-two-important
-strategies-for-speeding-up-your-reading/.

Newsletters, Feeds, and Podcasts

Alang, Navneet. "Information overload and why e-mail newsletters made
a comeback." *The Globe and Mail,* May 26, 2014, http://www.theglobe
andmail.com/technology/digital-culture/information-overload-and-why
-e-mail-newsletters-made-a-comeback/article18820835/.

Alexander, Bryan. "Future Trends in Technology and Education." Accessed December 6, 2016. https://bryanalexander.org/future-trends -in-technology-and-education/.

Hennig, Nicole. "Mobile Apps News." Accessed December 6, 2016. http://nicolehennig.com/mobile-apps-news/.

Hennig, Nicole. *Podcast Literacy: Recommending the Best Educational, Diverse, and Accessible Podcasts for Library Users.* Library Technology Reports 53, no. 2. Chicago: American Library Association, 2017. http:// nicolehennig.com/podcast-literacy/

Levine, Alaina G. "How to use Twitter to enhance your conference experience." *Physics Today,* March 16, 2016, http://scitation.aip.org/ content/aip/magazine/physicstoday/news/10.1063/PT.5.9054.

McManus, Richard. "Why following people on Twitter is broken (and what to do about it)." May 12, 2015, https://richardmacmanus .com/2015/05/12/twitter-follow/.

Dealing with Constant Change

Davidson, Cathy N. *Now You See It: How Technology and Brain Science Will Transform Schools and Business for the 21st Century.* London: Penguin, 2012.

Thomas, Douglas and John Seely Brown. *A New Culture of Learning: Cultivating the Imagination for a World of Constant Change.* Lexington, KY: CreateSpace, 2011. See also the book's website: http://www.newcultureoflearning.com/.

Unconferences

Buchanan, Leigh. "Welcome to the Unconference: why more industry associations and trade groups are letting members organize their own free-form unconferences." *Inc,* December 1, 2009, http://www.inc.com/ magazine/20091201/welcome-to-the-unconference.html.

Hamlin, Kaliya. "unConferencing – how to prepare to attend an unconference." Accessed December 6, 2016, http://unconference.net/ unconferencing-how-to-prepare-to-attend-an-unconference/.

Trend Reports

ALA Center for the Future of Libraries. "Trends." Accessed December 6, 2016, http://www.ala.org/transforminglibraries/future/trends.

Gartner. "Gartner's Hype Cycle." Accessed December 6, 2016, http://www.gartner.com/technology/research/methodologies/hype-cycle.jsp.

If you don't have institutional access to this expensive report, you can still find plenty of information in the press by searching for articles that mention it each year.

LITA: A Division of the American Library Association. "Top Technology Trends." Accessed December 6, 2016, http://www.ala.org/lita/about/committees/lit-ttt.

Meeker, Mary. "Internet Trends Report." Kleiner Perkins Caufield & Byers. Accessed December 6, 2016, http://www.kpcb.com/internet-trends.

MIT Technology Review. "10 Breakthrough Technologies." Accessed December 6, 2016, https://www.technologyreview.com/lists/technologies/2016/.

New Media Consortium. "NMC Horizon Reports." Accessed December 6, 2016, http://www.nmc.org/publication-type/horizon-report/. In addition to the other reports, look for each new year's library edition.

Pew Research Center. "Internet, Science & Tech." Accessed December 6, 2016, http://www.pewinternet.org. See their presentations page for useful summaries of recent data, http://www.pewinternet.org/category/presentations/.

PSFK. "Trend Reports." Accessed December 6, 2016, http://www.psfk.com/reports.

See also their summary slide decks, http://www.slideshare.net/psfk, and free trend briefings: http://trendwatching.com/freepublications/.

Rogers, Everett M. *Diffusion of Innovations*. New York: Free Press, 2005.

TrendWatching. "TrendWatching." Accessed December 6, 2016, http://trendwatching.com and http://trendwatching.com/freepublications/.

Webb, Amy. "8 Tech Trends to Watch in 2016." *Harvard Business Review,* December 8, 2015, https://hbr.org/2015/12/8-tech-trends-to-watch-in-2016. Search for a new version of this report in December of each year.

Books Summaries and How to Retain What You Read

Lee, Kevan. "Warren Buffett's Best Kept Secret to Success: The Art of Reading, Remembering, and Retaining More Books." Accessed

December 6, 2016, https://open.buffer.com/how-to-read-more-and
-remember-it-all/.

Book summary sites:

- "Blinkist." Accessed December 6, 2016, https://www.blinkist.com/.
  A paid subscription service which creates 2-minute reads based
  on key messages of each book.

- "Actionable Books." Accessed December 6, 2016, http://
  www.actionablebooks.com/. A free book summary site.

- "Deconstructing Excellence." Accessed December 6, 2016, http://
  www.deconstructingexcellence.com/. Book summary site that covers
  books on the topic of how to be a top performer in any field.

Learning from Popular Culture and Science Fiction

Finn, Ed & Kathryn Cramer. *Hieroglyph: Stories & Visions for a Better
Future*. New York: William Morrow, 2014. See also the book's website.
Accessed December 6, 2016, http://hieroglyph.asu.edu/book/hieroglyph/.

Marshall, Elizabeth and Özlem Sensoy. "Rethinking Popular Culture and
Media." Accessed December 6, 2016, http://www.rethinkingschools.org/
publication/rpcm/rpcm_intro.shtml.

McManus, Richard. "3 Reasons Why You Should Read Science Fiction."
September 1, 2016, https://richardmacmanus.com/2016/09/01/read
-science-fiction/.

Newitz, Annalee. "Dear Science Fiction Writers: Stop Being So
Pessimistic!" *Smithsonian Magazine,* April 2012, http://www.smith
sonianmag.com/science-nature/dear-science-fiction-writers-stop-being
-so-pessimistic-127226686/?no-ist.

Purdy, Patrick. "From Science Fiction to Science Fact: How Design Can
Influence the Future." *UX: User Experience, The Magazine of the User
Experience Professionals Association,* June 2013, http://uxpamagazine
.org/science-fiction-to-science-fact/.

Sawyer, Robert. "The Purpose of Science Fiction." *Slate*, January 27,
2011, http://www.slate.com/articles/technology/future_tense/2011/01/
the_purpose_of_science_fiction.html.

Shedroff, Nathan and Christopher Noessel. *Make It So: Interaction
Design Lessons from Science Fiction.* Brooklyn, NY: Rosenfeld
Media, 2012.

Kotler, Steven. *Tomorrowland: Our Journey from Science Fiction to Science Fact*. Boston: New Harvest, Houghton Mifflin Harcourt, 2015.

Wayne, Rachel. "Why it's important to study popular culture." July 27, 2014, https://www.linkedin.com/pulse/20140727233003-19409547 -why-it-s-important-to-study-pop-culture.

"Why Society Needs Science Fiction." *The Star Garden*. Accessed December 6, 2016, http://www.thestargarden.co.uk/Why-society -needs-science-fiction.html.

Ethical Debates

Al-Rodhan, Navef. "The Many Ethical Implications of Emerging Technologies." *Scientific American,* March 15, 2013, https://www .scientificamerican.com/article/the-many-ethical-implications-of -emerging-technologies/.

EFF: Electronic Frontier Foundation. "Surveillance Self-Defense: Tips, Tools and How-tos for Safer Online Communications." Accessed December 6, 2016, https://ssd.eff.org/. See also much more relevant information technology ethics on the EFF website, https://www.eff.org.

EPIC: Electronic Privacy Information Center. Accessed December 6, 2016, https://epic.org/. An excellent website for keeping up with privacy issues.

Fister, Barbara. "Weapons of Math Destruction: The Dark Side of Big Data." Review of a book of the same title by Cathy O'Neil. *Inside Higher Ed,* September 21, 2016, https://www.insidehighered.com/blogs/library -babel-fish/weapons-math-destruction-dark-side-big-data. Fisters' articles and book reviews for *Inside Higher Ed,* often focus on ethical debates around new technologies. Find her articles here, https://www .insidehighered.com/users/barbara-fister.

Franklin, Ursula. *The Real World of Technology (CBC Massey Lectures)*. Toronto: Anansi, 2004. See also audio recordings of her lectures, http:// www.cbc.ca/radio/ideas/the-1989-cbc-massey-lectures-the-real-world-of- technology-1.2946845.

John J. Reilly Center at the University of Notre Dame. "Emerging Ethical Dilemmas." Published each year, http://reilly.nd.edu/. For example, see 2016, http://reillytop10.com/. See also 2013, 2014, and 2015 for interesting ethical issues about new technologies that are still relevant.

2013, http://reilly.nd.edu/outreach/emerging-ethical-dilemmas-and
-policy-issues-in-science-and-technology/.

2014, http://reilly.nd.edu/outreach/emerging-ethical-dilemmas-and
-policy-issues-in-science-and-technology-2014/.

2015, http://reilly.nd.edu/outreach/emerging-ethical-dilemmas-and
-policy-issues-in-science-and-technology-2015/.

Diversity

American Library Association's Office for Diversity. "Strategic Planning
for Diversity." Accessed December 6, 2016, http://www.ala.org/advocacy/
diversity/workplace/diversityplanning.

Association of College and Research Libraries. "Diversity Standards:
Cultural Competency for Academic Libraries (2012)." Accessed
December 6, 2016, http://www.ala.org/acrl/standards/diversity.

Code{4}Lib Journal: Special Issue on Diversity in Library Technology.
Issue 28, April 15, 2015, http://journal.code4lib.org/issues/issues/
issue28.

Marcus, Bonnie. "The Lack of Diversity in Tech Is a Cultural Issue."
Forbes, August 12, 2015, http://www.forbes.com/sites/bonniemarcus/
2015/08/12/the-lack-of-diversity-in-tech-is-a-cultural-issue/
#60519ea63577.

McGee, Suzanne. "Why are 'innovative' tech companies still struggling
with diversity?" *The Guardian*. April 10, 2016, https://www.theguardian
.com/technology/us-money-blog/2016/apr/10/tech-diversity-companies
-recruiting-hiring.

*Model View Culture: A Magazine about Technology, Culture, and
Diversity.* Accessed December 6, 2016, https://modelviewculture.com/.

Salo, Dorothea. "Course syllabus, LIS 640: Code and Power." Accessed
December 6, 2016, http://dsalo.info/pdfs/uploads/2016/01/
640CodePowersyll2015.pdf.

Accessibility

BridgingApps. "Bridging Apps: Bridging the Gap between Technology
and People with Disabilities." Accessed December 6, 2016, http://
bridgingapps.org.

FCC: Federal Communications Commission. "Twenty-First Century Communications and Video Accessibility Act." Accessed December 6, 2016, http://www.fcc.gov/encyclopedia/twenty-first-century -communications-and-video-accessibility-act-0. Information about the 2010 law addressing captioning, audio description, and mobile browsers.

Horton, Sarah and Whitney Quesenbery. *A Web for Everyone: Designing Accessible User Experiences*. Brooklyn, NY: Rosenfeld Media, 2013.

Kowalsky, Michelle and John Woodruff. *Creating Inclusive Library Environments: A Planning Guide for Serving Patrons with Disabilities*. Chicago: ALA Editions, 2017.

Law Office of Lainey Feingold. "Digital Accessibility Laws around the Globe." May 9, 2013 and updated on March 29, 2016, http:// www.lflegal.com/2013/05/gaad-legal/.

Smith, Kel. *Digital Outcasts: Moving Technology Forward without Leaving People Behind*. Waltham, MA: Morgan Kaufmann, 2013.

Utah State University. "Web AIM: Web Accessibility in Mind." Accessed December 6, 2016, http://webaim.org/.

Digital Divide

Pew Research Center. Internet, Science & Tech. "Digital Divide." Accessed December 6, 2016, http://www.pewinternet.org/topics/ digital-divide/.

Pew Research Center. Internet, Science & Tech. "Emerging Technology Impacts." Accessed December 6, 2016, http://www.pewinternet.org/ topics/emerging-technology-impacts/.

West, Jessamyn C. *Without a Net: Librarians Bridging the Digital Divide*. Santa Barbara, CA: Libraries Unlimited, 2011. See also the book's website, http://www.librarian.net/digitaldivide/.

User Experience and User Needs Research

Baxter, Kathy and Catherine Courage and Kelly Caine. *Understanding Your Users: A Practical guide to User Research Methods*. Waltham, MA: Morgan Kaufmann, 2015. If you have access to Safari Books Online, this book is available there, https://www.safaribooksonline.com.

Bell, Steven. "Designing Better Libraries." Accessed December 6, 2016, http://dbl.lishost.org/blog/. An excellent blog by Steven Bell (http://stevenbell.info/) about user experience, design thinking, and creativity for libraries.

Buley, Leah. *The User Experience Team of One: A Research and Design Survival Guide.* Brooklyn, NY: Rosenfeld Media, 2013.

Fried Foster, Nancy. *Studying Students: A Second Look.* Chicago: Association of College and Research Libraries, a division of the American Library Association, 2013.

Fried Foster, Nancy. *Scholarly Practice, Participatory Design and the eXtensible Catalog.* Chicago: Association of College and Research Libraries, 2011.

Gabridge, Tracy, Millicent Gaskell, and Amy Stout. "Information Seeking through Students' Eyes: The MIT Photo Diary Study." *College and Research Libraries,* November 2008, http://crl.acrl.org/content/69/6/510.full.pdf.

Hennig, Nicole. "Academic E-Reading: Themes from User Experience Studies." Presentation at Society of Scholarly Publishers event on November 8, 2011 in Washington, DC. Accessed December 6, 2016, http://www.slideshare.net/nic221/academic-ereading-themes-from-user-experience-studies. See also "2011 Digital Scholarship Study: An Executive Summary." MIT Libraries User Experience Group, October 2011, http://hennigweb.com/keeping-up/dig-scholarship-summary.pdf. Download a copy of the cards we made to present to our staff about the themes of this study, http://hennigweb.com/keeping-up/ux-theme-cards.pdf.

Hennig, Nicole. "Students World: Photo Diary Study." Presentation at Computers in Libraries, April 16, 2007. http://www.slideshare.net/nic221/students-world-photo-diary-study

Priestner, Andy and Matt Borg. *User Experience in Libraries: Applying Ethnography and Human-Centred Design.* New York, NY: Routledge, 2016. See also their website, http://uxlib.org, which offers news of their conferences and events.

Schofield, Michael and Amanda L. Goodman. "LibUX," http://libux.co/. The authors of this website provides design and development consultancy for user experience departments and library web teams. Their site offers articles and podcast episodes about UX in libraries. They also manage a channel on Slack called LibUX,https://libraryux.slack.com.

Smashing Magazine. *A Field Guide to User Research*. Freiburg, Germany: Smashing Magazine, 2015. Kindle edition, https://www.amazon.com/Field-Guide-Research-Smashing-eBooks-ebook/dp/B00XOVIUJU.

UXPA: User Experience Professionals Association. "Definitions of User Experience and Usability." Accessed December 6, 2016, https://uxpa.org/resources/definitions-user-experience-and-usability.

Weave: Journal of Library User Experience. Accessed December 6, 2016, http://weaveux.org/. Weave is an open-access, peer-reviewed journal for library user experience professionals published by Michigan Publishing.

Fear of New Technologies

Bell, Vaughan. "Don't Touch That Dial! A History of Media Technology Scares, from the Printing Press to Facebook." *Slate*, February 15, 2010, http://www.slate.com/articles/health_and_science/science/2010/02/dont_touch_that_dial.single.html.

Wilson, Len. "11 Examples of Fear and Suspicion of New Technology." Accessed December 6, 2016, http://lenwilson.us/11-examples-of-fear-and-suspicion-of-new-technology/.

Letting Ideas Percolate

Reilly, Lucas. "Why Do Our Best Ideas Come to Us in the Shower?" *Mental Floss*, September 6, 2013, http://mentalfloss.com/article/52586/why-do-our-best-ideas-come-us-shower.

"Science of Daydreaming." *Dartmouth Undergraduate Journal of Science,* February 3, 2011, http://dujs.dartmouth.edu/2011/02/science-of-daydreaming/#.WBT6uOErLdR.

Note-Taking Practices

Busche, Laura. "50+ Awesome Resources to Create Visual Notes, Graphic Recordings & Sketchnotes." *Creative Market,* May 2, 2016, https://creativemarket.com/blog/50-awesome-resources-to-create-visual-notes-graphic-recordings-sketchnotes.

Buzan, Tony and Barry Buzan. *The Mind Map Book: How to Use Radiant Thinking to Maximize Your Brain's Untapped Potential.* New York: Dutton, 1994.

Buzan, Tony. *The Ultimate Book of Mind Maps: Unlock Your Creativity, Boost Your Memory, Change Your Life.* London: Harper Thorsons, 2005.

Roam, Dan. *Unfolding the Napkin: The Hands-On Method for Solving Complex Problems with Simple Pictures.* New York: Portfolio, 2009.

Rhode, Mike. *The Sketchnote Workbook: Advanced Techniques for Taking Visual Notes You Can Use Anywhere.* San Francisco, CA: Peachpit Press, 2015.

Rhode, Mike. *The Sketchnote Handbook: The Illustrated Guide to Visual Note Taking.* San Francisco, CA: Peachpit Press, 2013. See also the author's website, http://rohdesign.com/.

Trend-Spotting

Higham, William and Kogan Page. *The Next Big Thing: Spotting and Forecasting Consumer Trends for Profit.* Philadelphia: Kogan Page, 2010.

Housel, Morgan. "When You Change the World and No One Notices." Collaborative Fund, September 3, 2016, http://www.collaborative fund.com/blog/when-you-change-the-world-and-no-one-notices.

Kelly, Kevin. *The Inevitable: Understanding the Twelve Technological Forces That Will Shape Our Future.* New York: Viking, 2016. See also the author's website, http://kk.org/books/the-inevitable/.

Mason, Henry, et al. *Trend-Driven Innovation: Beat Accelerating Customer Expectations.* Hoboken, NJ: Wiley, 2015.

Rasmus, Daniel W. and Rob Salkowitz. *Listening to the Future: Why It's Everybody's Business.* Hoboken, NJ: Wiley, 2015.

Sakunthala. "High tech cool hunting." Software Is Eating the World, accessed December 6, 2016, https://medium.com/software-is-eating-the -world/high-tech-coolhunting-8b55879ea436#.df6dddy0x.

Schatsky, David. *Signals for Strategists: Sensing Emerging Trends in Business and Technology.* San Francisco: RosettaBooks, 2015.

Tetlock, Philip E. and Dan Dardner. *Superforecasting: The Art and Science of Prediction.* New York: Crown Publishers, 2015.

Project Methods: Design Thinking, Agile, and Lean Startup

Beck, Kent, et al. "Agile Software Development Manifesto," http://agilemanifesto.org.

Baker-Young, Melissa J. "Agile-like." M Library Blogs, November 22, 2016, http://www.lib.umich.edu/blogs/library-tech-talk/agile.

Bell, Steven. "Tipping Point for Design Thinking in Libraries (finally..?)" Accessed December 6, 2016, http://dbl.lishost.org/blog/2016/09/30/tipping-point-for-design-thinking-in-libraries-finally/.

Brown, Tim. *Change by Design: How Design Thinking Transforms Organizations and Inspires Innovation.* New York, NY: HarperCollins, 2009.

Cooper-Wright, Matt. "The Blurring Between Design Thinking and Agile." Frontline Interaction Design, November 23, 2016, https://medium.com/front-line-interaction-design/the-blurring-between-design-thinking-and-agile-ae59d14f28e3.

Fried, Jason. *Getting Real: The Smarter, Faster, Easier Way to Build a Successful Web Application.* S.l.: 37Signals, 2006. See also the website for this book. Accessed December 6, 2016, http://gettingreal.37signals.com/.

Gothelf, Jeff and Josh Seiden. *Lean UX: Applying Lean Principles to Improve User Experience.* Sebastopol, CA: O'Reilly Media, 2016.

IDEO. "Design Thinking for Libraries: A Toolkit for Patron-Centered Design." December, 31, 2014, http://designthinkingforlibraries.com/. Download the three documents linked from this site, "Toolkit Guide," http://designthinkingforlibraries.com/downloads/Libraries-Toolkit _2015.pdf, "Toolkit Activities Workbook," http://designthinking forlibraries.com/downloads/Libraries-Toolkit_Activities_2015.pdf, and "At-a-Glance Guide," http://designthinkingforlibraries.com/downloads/Libraries-Toolkit_At-a-Glance_2015.pdf.

IDEO. "Design Thinking for Educators." April 2013, http://www.designthinkingforeducators.com.

Martin, Roger L. *Design of Business: Why Design Thinking Is the Next Competitive Advantage.* Boston, MA: Harvard Business Press, 2009.

Ries, Eric. *The Lean Startup: How Constant Innovation Creates Radically Successful Businesses.* London: Portfolio Penguin, 2011. See also the website for this book, http://theleanstartup.com/, especially "Methodology," http://theleanstartup.com/principles.

Verdant, Roberto. *Design Driven Innovation: Changing the Rules of Competition by Radically Innovating What Things Mean.* Boston, MA: Harvard Business Press, 2009.

Ideation

Frey, Chuck. "The 7 All-Time Greatest Ideation Techniques." Innovation Management. Accessed December 6, 2016, http://www.innovationmanagement.se/2013/05/30/the-7-all-time-greatest-ideation-techniques/.

Gray, Dave. *Gamestorming: A Playbook for Innovators, Rulebreakers, and Changemakers.* Sebastopol, CA: O'Reilly, 2010.

Mattimore, Bryan W. *Idea Stormers: How to Lead and Inspire Creative Breakthroughs.* San Francisco, CA: Jossey-Bass, 2012.

Hennig, Nicole. "Innovation Smoothies." A Pecha Kucha talk for Internet Librarian, October 28, 2009, http://www.slideshare.net/nic221/innovation-smoothies-oct28.

Hohmann, Luke. *Innovation Games: Creating Breakthrough Products through Collaborative Play.* Upper Saddle River, NJ: Addison-Wesley, 2007.

Mattimore, Bryan W. *Idea Stormers: How to Lead and Inspire Creative Breakthroughs.* San Francisco, CA: Jossey-Bass, 2012.

Michalko, Michael. *Cracking Creativity: The Secrets of Creative Genius.* Berkeley, CA: Ten Speed Press, 2001.

Michalko, Michael. *Thinkertoys: A Handbook of Creative-Thinking Techniques.* Berkeley, CA: Ten Speed Press, 2006. There is also a card deck available with the methods in this book printed on each card, *Thinkpak: A Brainstorming Card Deck.* Berkeley, CA: Ten Speed Press, 2006.

Murnaw, Stefan, et al. *Caffeine for the Creative Team: 200 Exercises to Inspire Group Innovation.* Cincinnati, OH: HOW Books, 2009.

Murnaw, Stefan. *Creative Boot Camp: Generate Ideas in Greater Quantity and Quality in 30 Days.* San Francisco, CA: New Riders, 2012.

"Reverse It." Design Games Facilitating Creativity, UX Mastery. Accessed December 6, 2016, http://www.designgames.com.au/reverse_it/.

Ridley, Matt. *The Evolution of Everything: How New Ideas Emerge.* New York, NY: Harper, 2015.

Riley, Robert. "The Lotus Blossom Creative Technique." Thought Egg. Accessed December 6, 2016, http://thoughtegg.com/lotus-blossom -creative-technique/.

Hands-On Play

Johnson, Steven. *Wonderland: How Play Made the Modern World.* New York, NY: Riverhead Books, 2016.

Libow Martinez, Sylvia and Gary Stager. *Invent To Learn: Making, Tinkering, and Engineering in the Classroom.* Torrance, CA: Constructing Modern Knowledge Press, 2013. See also the website for this book, http://inventtolearn.com/.

McGonigal, Jane. *Reality Is Broken: Why Games Make Us Better and How They Can Change the World.* New York, NY: Penguin Press, 2011.

Mitra, Sugata. *Beyond the Hole in the Wall: Discover the Power of Self-Organized Learning.* New York, NY: Ted Conferences, 2012.

Wagner, Tony. *Creating Innovators: The Making of Young People Who Will Change the World.* New York, NY: Scribner, 2012.

Designing Tech Experiments

Design Brooklyn. "How to beta test your website." Accessed December 20, 2016, https://www.designbrooklyn.com/resources/help -center/How-to-Build-a-Website/How-to-Beta-Test-Your-Website.html.

Harvard University. "The Library Innovation Lab." Accessed December 20, 2016, http://lil.law.harvard.edu/.

MIT Libraries. "Experiments at the MIT Libraries." Accessed December 20, 2016, http://libraries.mit.edu/about/experiments/.

Sims, Peter. *Little Bets: How Breakthrough Ideas Emerge from Small Discoveries.* New York: Free Press, 2011.

Persuasion

Cialdini, Robert B. *Influence: The Psychology of Persuasion.* New York, NY: Collins, 2007.

Goldstein, Noah J., Steve J. Martin, and Robert B. Cialdini. *Yes!: 50 Scientifically Proven Ways to Be Persuasive.* New York, NY: Free Press, 2010.

Grenny, Joseph, et al. *Influencer: The New Science of Leading Change.* New York, NY: McGraw-Hill Education, 2013.

Heath, Dan and Chip Heath. *Switch: How to Change Things When Change Is Hard.* New York, NY: Broadway Books, 2010.

Heath, Dan and Chip Heath. *Made to Stick: Why Some Ideas Survive and Others Die.* New York, NY: Random House, 2008.

Sutton, Robert I. *Weird Ideas That Work.* New York, NY: Free Press, 2002.

Presenting

Anderson, Chris. *TED Talks: The Official TED Guide to Public Speaking.* Boston: Houghton Mifflin Harcourt, 2016.

Duarte, Nancy. *Slide:ology: The Art and Science of Creating Great Presentations.* Sebastopol, CA: O'Reilly Media, 2008.

Duarte, Nancy. *Resonate: Present Visual Stories that Transform Audiences.* Hoboken, NJ: Wiley, 2010.

Duarte, Nancy. *Illuminate: Ignite Change Through Speeches, Stories, Ceremonies, and Symbols.* New York, NY: Portfolio/Penguin, 2016. See also the author's website, http://www.duarte.com/perspective/#books.

Gallo, Carmine. *The Presentation Secrets of Steve Jobs: How to Be Insanely Great in Front of Any Audience.* New York, NY: McGraw-Hill, 2010.

Redish, Janice (Ginny). *Letting Go of the Words: Writing Web Content That Works.* Boston, MA: Elsevier/Morgan Kaufmann Publishers, 2007.

Roam, Dan. *The Back of the Napkin (Expanded Edition): Solving Problems and Selling Ideas with Pictures.* New York, NY: Portfolio, 2010.

Roam, Dan. *Draw to Win: A Crash Course on How to Lead, Sell, and Innovate With Your Visual Mind.* New York, NY: Portfolio, 2016.

Job Descriptions and Hiring

Adler, Lou. *Hire with Your Head: Using Performance-based Hiring to Build Great Teams.* Hoboken, NJ: John Wiley & Sons, 2007.

Adler, Lou. "Performance-based Hiring is Your Best Bet for Diverse Hiring." LinkedIn Talent Blog, June 16, 2015, https://business.linkedin .com/talent-solutions/blog/2015/06/performance-based-hiring-is-your -best-bet-for-diverse-hiring.

FGP: Find Great People. "How to Develop Performance Based Objectives." Accessed December 6, 2016, http://www.fgp.com/ knowledge-center/client-resources/how-to-develop-performance -based-objectives.

Hewlett, Sylvia Ann, Melinda Marshall, and Laura Sherbin. "How Diversity Can Drive Innovation." *Harvard Business Review,* December 2013, https://hbr.org/2013/12/how-diversity-can-drive -innovation.

Hunt, Vivian, Dennis Layton, and Sara Prince. "Why Diversity Matters." McKinsey & Company, February 2015, http://www.mckinsey.com/ business-functions/organization/our-insights/why-diversity-matters.

Lou Adler Group. "Performance based Hiring." Accessed December 6, 2016, http://louadlergroup.com/about-us/performance-based-hiring/.

Luddbrarian, The. "Will Technological Critique Emerge with Emerging Technology Librarians?" LibrarianShipwreck. Accessed December 6, 2016, https://librarianshipwreck.wordpress.com/2013/07/30/will -technological-critique-emerge-with-emerging-technology-librarians/.

Overaa, Jennifer M. "Emerging Career Trends for Information Professionals:

A Snapshot of Job Postings Spring 2016." SJSU School of Information. Slide deck. Accessed December 6, 2016, http://ischool.sjsu.edu/sites/ default/files/content_pdf/career_trends.pdf.

Radniecki, Tara. "Study on Emerging Technologies Librarians: How a new library position and its competencies are evolving to meet the technology and information needs of libraries and their patrons." Paper presented at: IFLA WLIC 2013—Singapore—Future Libraries: Infinite Possibilities in Session 152—Reference and Information Services. Accessed December 6, 2016, http://library.ifla.org/134/.

Rose, Todd. "How Job Descriptions Undermine the Hiring Process." *Fast Company,* January 19, 2016, https://www.fastcompany.com/ 3055044/work-smart/how-job-descriptions-undermine-your-hiring -process.

Sullivan, John. "7 Rules for Job Interview Questions That Result in Great Hires." *Harvard Business Review,* February 10, 2016, https://hbr.org/2016/02/7-rules-for-job-interview-questions-that-result-in-great-hires.

Library Innovation and the Future

Fishman Lipsey, Rebecca. "100 Great Ideas for the Future of Libraries—A New Paradigm for Civic Engagement." The Huffington Post, March 31, 2015, http://www.huffingtonpost.com/rebecca-fishman-lipsey/100-great-ideas-for-the-for-the-future-of-libraries_b_6551440.html. Full report available here, https://www.dropbox.com/sh/bms756giuec7rir/AABpQpM9vJjDVqL7cYU6rncua?dl=0&preview=100GreatIdeas_FutureofLibraries.pdf.

Journal of Library Innovation. Accessed December 6, 2016, http://www.libraryinnovation.org/. This journal ceased publication after the fall 2015 issue, but there is still plenty of good content available on the website and through aggregated databases that indexed this journal.

Knight Foundation. "Future of Libraries." Accessed December 6, 2016, http://www.knightfoundation.org/topics/future-of-libraries.

Molaro, Anthony and Leah L. White, editors. *The Library Innovation Toolkit: Ideas, Strategies, and Programs.* Chicago: ALA Editions, an imprint of the American Library Association, 2015.

Putnam, Laurie. "How Can We Support Library Innovation?" Mediashift, November 2015, http://mediashift.org/2015/11/how-can-we-support-library-innovation/. See also the author's blog, NextLibraries, http://www.nextlibraries.org/, and her bookmarks, "LibraryFutures," https://del.icio.us/LibraryFutures.

Zickuhr, Kathryn. "Innovative library services 'in the wild.'" Pew Internet, January 29, 2013, http://libraries.pewinternet.org/2013/01/29/innovative-library-services-in-the-wild.

Books about Emerging Technologies for Libraries

These books focus on specific technologies.

Burke, John J. *The Neal-Schuman Library Technology Companion, Fifth Edition: A Basic Guide for Library Staff.* Chicago: Neal-Schuman, an imprint of the American Library Association, 2016.

Koerber, Jennifer and Michael Sauers. *Emerging Technologies: A Primer for Librarians.* Lanham, MD: Rowman & Littlefield, 2015.

Kroski, Ellyssa. *The Tech Set #1–10.* New York, NY: Neal-Schuman, 2010.

Kroski, Ellyssa. *The Tech Set #11–20.* Chicago: Lita, ALA TechSource, 2012.

A series of guides about specific technologies.

Varnum, Kenneth J., author and editor. *The Top Technologies Every Librarian Needs to Know: A LITA Guide.* Chicago: American Library Association, 2014.

Yan, Sharon Q. *Emerging Technologies for Librarians: A Practical Approach to Innovation.* Waltham, MA: Chandos, 2015.

Guide to Mobile Apps

The following is a list of recommended apps for doing the different kinds of work discussed in this book. More information about each app is found throughout this book in the chapter of the corresponding name.

All of the apps in this list have versions for both iOS and Android unless otherwise indicated. Most of them also have web versions and some have versions for Mac or Windows. If any of the links below don't work, search for the app in Apple's app store (for iOS), or the Google Play Store (for Android).

You can do much of this work on the go, using your mobile device. The best apps can sync back to your desktop or laptop so that you can continue your work there. See also my list of "50 Best Apps for Those Who Use Both Android and iOS," http://nicolehennig.com/50-best-apps-use -android-ios/, which discusses the best apps that keep their information synchronized across your devices.

Subscribing to Newsletters, Feeds, and Groups

Blog feeds and social writing platforms

- Feedly, https://feedly.com
- Medium, https://medium.com/m/app

Groups and communities

- Google+, https://www.google.com/mobile/+/
- Facebook, https://www.facebook.com/mobile/
- Reddit app, https://www.reddit.com/r/redditmobile/
- Slack app, https://slack.com/downloads/

Visual sources

- Pinterest, https://www.pinterest.com/
- Instagram, https://www.instagram.com
- Slideshare, http://www.slideshare.net/mobile_app_promo

Following people and organizations

- Twitter, https://twitter.com/download
- Hootsuite, https://hootsuite.com/products/mobile-apps
- Tweetdeck, https://about.twitter.com/products/tweetdeck
- Buffer, https://buffer.com/
- Nuzzle, http://nuzzel.com/

Multimedia Resources: Video, Audio, and Courses
Video

- YouTube, https://www.youtube.com/yt/devices/
- Vimeo, https://vimeo.com/everywhere

Courses

- iTunes U, http://www.apple.com/education/itunes-u/ (iOS only)
- Coursera, https://www.coursera.org/about/mobile
- EdX, https://www.edx.org/mobile
- *Lynda.com*, https://www.lynda.com/apps

Podcasts

- Pocket Casts, https://www.shiftyjelly.com/pocketcasts/
- Overcast, https://overcast.fm/ (iOS only)

- Castro, http://supertop.co/castro/

- Otto Radio, https://www.ottoradio.com/

- Downcast, http://www.downcastapp.com/ (iOS only)

- BeyondPod, https://www.beyondpod.mobi/android/index.htm (Android only)

- Stitcher, https://www.stitcher.com/download.php

Narration

- Capti Voice Narrator, https://www.captivoice.com

Dealing with Information Overload

Quickly process your e-mail

- Newton, https://cloudmagic.com/k/newton

- Spark, https://sparkmailapp.com/ (iOS only)

- Inbox by Gmail, https://www.google.com/inbox/

Save articles to read later

- Pocket, https://getpocket.com

- Instapaper, https://www.instapaper.com/apps

Automate your information flow

- IFTTT, https://ifttt.com/

- Zapier, https://zapier.com/ (web only)

- Google Alerts, https://www.google.com/alerts

- Mention, https://mention.com/en/download-apps/

- Hooks, http://www.gethooksapp.com/

Backups

- CrashPlan, https://support.code42.com/CrashPlan/4/Restoring/ CrashPlan_Mobile_App

(See "Why I prefer CrashPlan for online backups," by Joe Kissell. *Macworld*, April 28, 2015, http://www.macworld.com/article/2915637/ why-i-prefer-crashplan-for-online-backups.html).

Conferences and Local Events

- Lanyrd, http://lanyrd.com/mobile/
- Meetup, https://www.meetup.com/apps/

Book-Reading

E-book readers

- Kindle, https://www.amazon.com/kindle-dbs/fd/kcp
- iBooks, http://www.apple.com/ibooks/ (iOS and MacOS only)
- MegaReader, http://www.megareader.net/ (iOS only)

Scan book barcodes

- Pic2Shop, http://www.pic2shop.com/

Book summaries

- Blinkist, https://www.blinkist.com/

Speed-reading

- Accelerator (iOS only), http://acceleratorapp.com/
- A Faster Reader (Android only), https://play.google.com/store/apps/details?id=com.basetis.blinkingread.blinkingread&hl=en

Gathering Information about User Needs

Recording user interviews

- iTalk Recorder, https://griffintechnology.com/us/italk-premium (iOS only)
- Just Press Record, http://www.openplanetsoftware.com/just-press-record/

Note-taking for user interviews and field studies

- See note-taking section below.

Note-Taking

Notes in multiple formats

- Evernote, https://www.evernote.com
- Microsoft One Note, https://www.onenote.com/

- Google Keep, https://keep.google.com
- Simple Note, https://simplenote.com/downloads/
- DayOne Journal, http://dayoneapp.com/

Mobile document scanning

- Genius Scan, http://www.thegrizzlylabs.com/genius-scan/
- JotNot Pro, http://www.jotnot.com/scanner.html
- Scanbot, https://scanbot.io/en/
- Scantastic, http://scantastic.smoca.ch/

Mind mapping

- Popplet, https://itunes.apple.com/US/app/id374151636?mt=8 (iOS only)
- SimpleMind, https://play.google.com/store/apps/details?id=com .modelmakertools.simplemindfree&hl=en (Android only)

Curating Information

- *Scoop.it*, http://www.scoop.it/apps
- Paper.li, http://paper.li/
- Mailchimp, https://mailchimp.com/features/mailchimp-mobile/
- Constant Contact, https://www.constantcontact.com/logout/mobile -apps
- TinyLetter, https://tinyletter.com/
- Pinterest, https://about.pinterest.com/en
- Teachable, https://teachable.com/
- Udemy, https://www.udemy.com/user/nicolehennig/, and teach a course, http://ude.my/ref01f

Trend Spotting

- *Hacker News*, https://news.ycombinator.com/
- *Stack Overflow*, http://stackoverflow.com/

Ideation

- *Brainstormer*, http://www.tapnik.com/brainstormer/ (iOS only)

Job Descriptions

- *LinkedIn*, https://mobile.linkedin.com/

- *Job Search—Simply Hired*, http://www.simplyhired.com/post-jobs
-free

- *Indeed*, http://www.indeed.com/mobile

To stay current with the best apps for education and productivity, subscribe to my newsletter, Mobile Apps News, http://nicolehennig .com/mobile-apps-news/.

Index

About the Author

NICOLE HENNIG is an independent user-experience professional, helping librarians and educators stay current with the best mobile technologies.

Her books include *Apps for Librarians: Using the Best Mobile Technology to Educate, Create, and Engage; Selecting and Evaluating the Best Mobile Apps for Library Services*; and *Mobile Learning Trends: Accessibility, Ecosystems, Content Creation.* See her other publications here: http://nicolehennig.com/books/.

She offers online courses and webinars, including *Apps for Librarians & Educators* and *Organize Your Life with Mobile Apps.* See her complete list of courses: http://nicolehennig.com/courses/ and webinars: http://nicolehennig.com/webinars.

She worked for the MIT Libraries for 14 years, first as web manager and then as head of the user experience department. She is the winner of several awards, including the *MIT Excellence Award for Innovative Solutions.* In 2013 she left to start her own business, teaching courses, offering webinars, and writing books and articles on new technologies for information professionals.

Nicole enjoys teaching, presenting, and inspiring people to use technology effectively. To stay current with the best mobile technologies for education and productivity, sign up for her e-mail newsletter, Mobile Apps News, and follow her on Twitter *@nic221*.